JAPAN
THE TOOTHLESS TIGER
Second Edition

To: Angela, Aidan, Brendan, Carmel, Kit, Mary.
Is Buaine Bláth Ná Saol.

DECLAN HAYES

JAPAN
THE TOOTHLESS TIGER

Second Edition

TUTTLE Publishing

Tokyo | Rutland, Vermont | Singapore

Published by Tuttle Publishing, an imprint
of Periplus Editions (HK) Ltd.

www.tuttlepublishing.com

LC control no.: 00053621

ISBN 978-4-8053-1304-6

Distributed by:

North America, Latin America & Europe
Tuttle Publishing
364 Innovation Drive, North Clarendon
VT 05759-9436, USA
Tel: 1 (802) 773 8930; Fax: 1 (802) 773 6993
info@tuttlepublishing.com
www.tuttlepublishing.com

Japan
Tuttle Publishing
Yaekari Building 3rd Floor
5-4-12 Osaki Shinagawa-ku
Tokyo 1410032, Japan
Tel: (81) 3 5437 0171; Fax: (81) 3 5437 0755
sales@tuttle.co.jp; www.tuttle.co.jp

Asia Pacific
Berkeley Books Pte Ltd
61 Tai Seng Avenue #02-12
Singapore 534167
Tel: (65) 6280 1330; Fax: (65) 6280 6290
inquiries@periplus.com.sg
www.periplus.com

16 15 14 13   5 4 3 2 1   1310MP

Printed in Singapore

TUTTLE PUBLISHING® is a registered
trademark of Tuttle Publishing, a division
of Periplus Editions (HK) Ltd.

The Tuttle Story
"Books to Span the East and West"

Many people are surprised to learn that the world's largest publisher of books on Asia had its humble beginnings in the tiny American state of Vermont. The company's founder, Charles E. Tuttle, belonged to a New England family steeped in publishing.

Immediately after WW II, Tuttle served in Tokyo under General Douglas MacArthur and was tasked with reviving the Japanese publishing industry. He later founded the Charles E. Tuttle Publishing Company, which thrives today as one of the world's leading independent publishers.

Though a westerner, Tuttle was hugely instrumental in bringing a knowledge of Japan and Asia to a world hungry for information about the East. By the time of his death in 1993, Tuttle had published over 6,000 books on Asian culture, history and art—a legacy honored by the Japanese emperor with the "Order of the Sacred Treasure," the highest tribute Japan can bestow upon a non-Japanese.

With a backlist of 1,500 titles, Tuttle Publishing is more active today than at any time in its past—inspired by Charles Tuttle's core mission to publish fine books to span the East and West and provide a greater understanding of each.

Contents

Preface to the Second Edition

Sometimes political events move quickly. An unforeseen event happens, things come to a head and those unforeseen events have unintended consequences. Eventually, a consensus of one form or another is re-established and longer term priorities and objectives reassert themselves.

That is because all nations, China and Japan included, have no permanent friends, only permanent interests. Because the permanent interests of China and Japan, East Asia's main protagonists, do not and cannot change, *Japan: The Toothless Tiger* is even more relevant now than when it was first published in 2001. This is because my analysis was, by and large, totally correct.

My book correctly outlines the growing hard and soft power of China before contending that Japan will have to make hard diplomatic and military choices as China continues to emerge from its supposed century of slumber and shame to reassert itself. Indeed, though China's expansionist aggression can be explained in the context of China's present and future social, industrial, and political interests, Japan's lethargy since this book first appeared is harder to explain away.

Though significant events have indeed happened—the 2004 deployment of Japanese ground troops to Iraq, the logistical support the Japanese Navy gave during the 2004 Asian tsunami and, from 2002 to 2010, for the war in Afghanistan as well as the 2013 placing of anti-missile batteries in Tokyo, all spring immediately to mind—underlying causes and tensions remain the same, as does Japan's stance, which still resembles that of a doomed deer in the Chinese headlights.

Thus, though Japan's presence in Iraq was significant, as it was the first time they had been deployed in a potential combat role since 1945, it was mostly symbolic and of no real strategic or tactical consequence. Japan presently cannot engage in overseas ground operations without the close political, military, and logistical support of her allies, the United States in particular. Not only has Japan not got that capability but China knows that, on land, Japan is very much a paper tiger and China has calculated accordingly as it gauges Japanese diplomatic, economic, and military resistance to its ongoing adventurism.

Though Japan's Iraq deployment was symbolically significant, Japan's response to the Asian tsunami was much more telling and much more relevant. Both the Japanese and Indians sent their blue water fleets into overseas waters and independently supplied them, something that is crucial in naval operations and something the Chinese failed miserably to do following the Asian tsunami.

But the Chinese Navy has not stood still. In its quest to turn the South China Sea into a Chinese lake, it continues to probe, to provoke and to improve its capability to a degree where it will soon stretch the Japanese, Indian, and Vietnamese navies to breaking point. The threat of China's rapidly increasing naval and military capability can be seen not only in the case of the waters China claims from Japan but, more starkly perhaps, also with the waters it seeks to annex from Vietnam and the Philippines, two countries with historically different perspectives on China.

Chinese aggression toward Vietnam, part of an ongoing 1000 year campaign at subjugating them, continues by land and by sea. Though the Vietnamese repelled the 1979 Chinese invasion, they are unlikely to keep the Chinese Army at bay forever; numbers and vast military expenditures by Beijing will see to that. China and Vietnam will remain at loggerheads, not least because of the overt racism of the Chinese who, in the words of Deng Xiaoping, the former Chinese leader, regard the Vietnamese (and Koreans) as disobedient children deserving chastisement, via the Chinese People's Liberation Army and the Chinese Navy which, in scenes mirroring those being played out in the Japanese waters bordering Okinawa, continues to prowl around Vietnam's Spratly Islands.

Although it could be said it was the Chinese parents and not the Vietnamese children who got their bottoms smacked in 1979, the longer term reasons for that war are worth considering, not only for their consequences to South East Asia but for Korea and Japan as well. Deng Xiaoping justified the Chinese attack by saying it was prompted by the Soviets' attempt "to extend its evil tentacles to Southeast Asia and...carry out expansion there" and that the Soviets were using China's "naughty Vietnamese children" (his words, not mine) as proxies to encircle the perennially suffering Chinese. Whatever the Soviets' intentions, those of the Chinese were quite clear. They attacked Vietnam to revert it into a vassal Chinese state and to show the Vietnamese that their Soviet allies could not effectively help them when faced with the might of the Chinese forces pitted against them. The Chinese even went so far as to mobilize millions of troops along the Soviet border to show the Vietnamese and their erstwhile allies they meant business. And, as this massive saber rattling was accompanied by actual attacks on Vietnam, China's threat of a full scale military war with the Soviet Union over Vietnam was not an idle bluff.

Vietnam has, of course, proved a notoriously difficult country to subjugate and the Vietnamese Navy, as of spring 2013, are still bravely, if somewhat forlornly, standing up to renewed Chinese aggression around their islands. Though Vietnam's navy faces insurmountable odds, they are not totally alone. Because India now finds herself suffering from Chinese aggression against Indian oil exploration companies in the same general area of the South

China Sea, Admiral D.K. Joshi, India's navy chief, has declared that, though India is not a territorial claimant in the South China Sea, its navy will take the necessary military action against China to protect its maritime and economic interests in Vietnam's waters. Though the United States, as well as Vietnam, Taiwan, the Philippines and several of the other countries claiming the Spratlys, have also voiced concern at China harassing international ships in these waters, the Chinese Navy plows on regardless, bullying big and small potential adversaries alike with reckless and irresponsible abandon.

China's aggressive intents can probably be best seen in its relationships with the relatively benign and harmless Philippines and with the more problematic Korea than it can with Vietnam, where it is truly loathed. Although the Philippines has enjoyed historically cordial relationships with China, China still treats them as another potential vassal state, as one more country and people that must be brought to heel in the same way that previous Chinese dynasties subdued Korea and Vietnam for centuries. Although the Philippines presents no military, economic or other threat whatsoever to China, the Chinese Navy still prowls her waters, annexing her off shore islands, including those within sight of inhabited Filipino islands, all for the Greater China policy. Because they have not the power or mettle to stand up to the Chinese aggressors, all the Philippines can do is hope that help will come from afar.

And China knows that that power from afar can only be one of a very small number of suspects, Japan and the United States being the most obvious, acting either alone or in concert. Indeed, as befitting a nation with a king-sized persecution complex, China needs a pantomime villain and Japan and Japanese history, suitably amended, fill that role admirably. Though we discuss it at length later, let's nail the most relevant part of Sino Japanese history here. As a result of the acceptance by the Japanese Imperial government on August 15, 1945 of the terms of the Potsdam

Declaration calling for the unconditional surrender of Japan, Lieut. Gen. Okamura Yasutsugu, Commander of Japanese Forces in Central China, surrendered his forces to those of Generalissimo Chiang Kai-shek, Supreme Commander of the Allied Forces in the China Theatre, whose representative also took the Japanese Tokyo Bay surrender on the USS *Missouri*. Because it is, in other words, the name of Chiang Kai-shek, not Mao Tse Tung, which appears on all of Japan's surrender documents, it is the Taiwanese and the 1911 Chinese Republic they swear allegiance to and not the ruling Communist Party of China, which commands the moral high ground in World War II and, that being so, the Chinese Communist Party should stop milking that particular cash cow. Mao's forces capitalized on the chaos in the aftermath of World War II in the same way the Nazis did from the chaos that engulfed Europe after the Great War. Mao simply extended his toe hold thanks to the confusion which ensued—and from the help of the 650,000 Soviet troops who invaded Manchuria in the dying days of the Japanese Empire. Because it was Chiang Kai-shek's forces which took the Japanese surrender and because Japan has already paid massive reparations in kind, the Communist Party of China has no unpaid claims on World War II. The Chinese side of that account has been paid in full even if not all of the payments went to the true victims or their Taiwanese and other representatives. China, along with its despicable vassal state of North Korea, should simply shut up about World War II and begin paying their own reparations for their own massive crimes against the Chinese and Korean people in the years following the collapse of Nationalist China.

Even if they conceded those obvious points, the Chinese Communist Party will argue that, though they did not win the war, they most certainly have won the peace. But what price peace? China is the force that keeps North Korea's Communist dynasty in power. And that is nothing to boast of. Since *Japan: The Toothless Tiger* was first published, millions more North Koreans have died of hunger and disease, hundreds of thousands more languish in North Korean gulags and, if the almost daily accounts of their activities are to be believed, the very strange Chinese puppets who control North Korea, when not engaged in starving their people to death, seem to spend their waking hours developing even more weapons of mass destruction to threaten South Korea and Japan with. And that, like the subjugation of Tibet, is nothing for the Chinese to boast of. If North Korea is their weather vane, China's leaders are very dangerous people indeed. If we are to judge countries by the company they keep and the alliances they maintain, China's umbilical link with North Korea must be not only one of the most despicable but one of the most cynical alliances in history.

The Chinese Communist Party will argue that they have lifted tens and even hundreds of millions of Chinese people out of poverty and, as that is something to boast of, "minor" issues like their rampant abuses in North Korea and Tibet are only inconsequential historical hiccups of no real consequence. And they have a point.

By any yardstick, the recent emergence of the People's Republic of China as a major world force has been spectacular. Even though saddled with 22 percent of the world's population and 7 percent of the world's cultivated land, China has shifted from being a net food importer to net food exporter since the mid 1980s. China's inexhaustible supply of cheap labor, its massive foreign exchange reserves and its ability to buy, develop, and reverse engineer more capital intensive production modes will continue to enhance China's position as Asia's rising economic hegemon.

The Chinese economy, for all its impressive growth, works under a number of long term constraints, the most critical of which is probably water, which is fundamental to any food system. Since water is a resource vital to life for which there is no substitute, the only choice to be made is how to allocate water, and how to find the most efficient way of using it.

Although 70 percent of the grain produced in China comes from irrigated land, the Middle Kingdom is seeing its irrigation supply depleted on three fronts: the diversion of water from rivers and reservoirs to cities; the depletion of underground supplies in aquifers; and the increasing pollution caused by rapid industrialization. Although there are 50,000 kilometers of major rivers in China, 80 percent of them are so degraded they no longer support fish. As a result of toxic discharge from cities and upstream enterprises, which include such highly polluting industries as paper mills, tanneries, oil-refineries and chemical plants, the average water availability is about 2,300 m³, which is roughly about one third of the world's average value.

But China's water resources are also unevenly distributed between the humid south and the more arid north: although North China has only about 20 percent of total water resources in China, it is supporting more than half of the total population. Whereas two-thirds of China's agriculture is in the North, four-fifths of its water is in the South. Of the five watersheds where most of the country's people and farms are concentrated, four—the Yellow, Liao, Hai, and Huai Rivers—are in the arid North; the Yellow River water is now so loaded with heavy metals and other toxins that it is unfit even for irrigation, much less for human consumption.

Even as the Yellow River, aquifers, and wells get drier, Chinese water demand continues to soar both in the agricultural and non agricultural sectors. As water competition among farms, homes, and industries intensifies, farms inevitably lose out. In those areas of North China where all available water is being used, these short-falls can be filled only by diverting water from agriculture, which cannot compete with industry in China or anywhere else. A thousand tons of water produces one ton of wheat, which has a market value of $200, whereas the same amount of water used in industry yields an estimated $14,000 of output—70 times as much. Moreover, that economic imperative is reinforced by China's political one: the need to provide jobs for some 14 million new entrants into the labor force each year; this is more easily and more profitably done in industry than in agriculture.

Though water is China's biggest long-term problem, securing petroleum and key minerals are more immediate ones and China is adopting very sinister means to meet her needs in those fields. The speed with which China's international petroleum activity has grown, the number and geographic distribution of their projects, the scale of available funds and the number of Chinese companies involved has transformed the global petroleum industry itself. Further, the close involvement of China's government in many of the projects, the frequency with which petroleum projects are integrated into a wider package of economic and political deals, and the reactionary political nature of many of the host governments continues to alarm the international community. Their concerns are exacerbated by the perceived international political ambitions of China's government and the country's own disreputable history both as a repressive Communist state and as an imperial hegemon.

Nor are water and petroleum the only causes for concern. China is a major producer of advanced technology products (ATPs), annually shipping about $50 billion, or 19 percent of all U.S. ATP goods to the United States; China is a major U.S. supplier of electronics, opto-electronics, as well as information and communications equipment. The U.S. imported $140 billion of advanced technology products from the China Sphere in 2004, which is 270 percent more than it imported from the European Union. China and ten of the nations surrounding it (the outer China Sphere) now supply 59 percent of all ATP products imported into the U.S. The China Sphere supplies the United States with 18 percent of all imported ATP Life Science products, 60 percent of opto-electronics, 77 percent of information and equipment ATP, 52 percent of electronics ATP, 53 percent of flexible manufacturing ATP, and 67 percent of advanced materials ATP. The U.S. ran a $60 billion ATP trade deficit with the China Sphere in 2004.

These ATPs depend on a small number of minerals, metals, and raw materials in which China is currently cornering the global market. Because China needs a steady supply of minerals, metals, oil and other raw materials to fuel its industries, to feed its population and to achieve her hegemonic goals, she is revolutionizing world demand for raw materials and changing the map of global competitiveness, most notably in strategic minerals. Of the 24 major non-fuel minerals consumed by industrial nations, the United States is substantially dependent on imports for 21 of them; because African nations, for example, are a major source of chromium, cobalt, manganese, platinum as well as bauxite, diamonds, and gold, China has been particularly active securing resources and allies there.

The availability of these minerals has an extremely important impact on American industry and in turn, on U.S. defense capabilities. Without just a few critical minerals, such as cobalt, manganese, chromium, and platinum, it would be virtually impossible to produce many defense products such as jet engines and missile components.

Virtually all the world's reserves of these strategic minerals lie either in the former Soviet Union, China or in Africa. Between them, these areas contain over 90 percent of the world's platinum, manganese, and chromium ores. If the supply of any of these stopped, the United States would have to rely on its stockpiled supply. This would only create a short term solution as the stockpiled amount would last for about three years, thus obviating the United States choosing a long term attrition strategy. This places the U.S. in a vulnerable position with a direct threat to her defense production capability if China could disrupt the secular supply of these strategic minerals. China herself now supplies approximately 95 percent of the world's rare earth minerals, a class of minerals with properties that make them essential for applications including miniaturized electronics, computer disk drives, display screens, missile guidance, pollution control catalysts, and advanced materials.

The Chinese strategy of mineral starvation could center around three courses of action. First, they could restrict the sale of their own minerals to the West. In recent years Chinese exports of several strategic minerals have been sharply curtailed or halted entirely. These actions have had the desired effect of tightening supplies and increasing the West's dependence on African supply sources. Chinese export quotas have also resulted in a dramatic shift in the world's rare earth knowledge base. As examples, the division of General Motors which deals with miniaturized magnet research closed its U.S. office and relocated its entire staff to China in 2006; Magnequench, a company formerly based in Valparaiso, Indiana, which manufactures roughly 80 percent of the rare-earth magnets used in building smart bombs, has also relocated to the Middle Kingdom, thereby giving China a strategic advantage in building powerful high-technology industries and modernizing its armed forces.

Secondly, the Chinese have moved into international markets competing with the West for their traditional sources of supply. The result is that they are conserving their own resources while limiting supplies available to the Western countries. The third course of action the Chinese have embarked upon is a program of extending their influence, particularly in Africa, but also in Latin America and other raw material sources.

Although China cannot currently militarily conquer Africa, she seeks essentially three things from Africa: unimpeded and virtually exclusive access to natural resources; new markets for her export-driven economy; and increased influence among international political bodies. Beijing's mercantilist strategy has been extremely successful largely because it is accompanied by a clear government policy in support of African commercial ventures, abundant financing and tax benefits for Chinese firms operating abroad, and robust diplomacy toward the region's most despicable regimes. Beijing, which poses as a non-imperialist power, propounds a non-interventionist policy and does not demand good governance, democracy, human rights or governmental transparency in human rights black spots such as Sudan and Zimbabwe, which are both closely allied with Beijing, and which routinely extends diplomatic protection to them at the United Nations and other forums where China has veto power. All of these factors have enabled China to establish strategic counterbalances designed to increase its power and limit that of the United States and her allies.

The idea that population, logistical and resource pressures, such as those now facing China, may lead governments to conquer overseas territories has been unpopular in the West for a long time for three reasons: firstly because levels of technological and economic development are far more important than population density in determining well-being; secondly because population growth may be controlled; and thirdly, and most infamously, because notions of *Lebensraum* played a central and invidious role in Nazi Germany's aggression of the 1930s and 1940s. Yet all the evidence suggests that precisely such ideas have strongly influenced Chinese policy in the South China Sea since the fall of Saigon to the North Vietnamese. China has been methodically colonizing the South China Sea by grabbing remote islands, building harbors, airfields, lighthouses, and barracks on them and using them as jumping off points to colonize more islands.

Chinese apologists farcically argue that these islands, some of which are within sight of the main islands of the rest of the Philippines and others of which had been integral parts of the Republic of South Vietnam, have always been integral parts of the Chinese empire; that the Chinese Navy must colonize them to prevent Vietnam or some other tributary state using them as launching pads to attack China; and that China needs the islands' fishing, mineral, and oil resources to maintain its economic growth and concomitant living space or *Lebensraum* for its people to achieve their manifest destiny.

China's naval adventurism is part of an established pattern of passive aggression which includes intimidating Russia, Japan, Vietnam, Tibet, and Taiwan and surrounding and undermining

India by use of conventional weapons, Assassin's Mace weapons and brute economic power. Given China's low cost strategic advantages and that the role of the hegemon is deeply woven into China's national identity, it is entirely theoretically and empirically legitimate to view China's aggression as that of a rising mercantilist hegemon.

Since *The Toothless Tiger* was first published, China's defense budget has mushroomed from a relatively modest $30bn in 2002 to over $200bn; at that rate of increase, its military spending will easily surpass that of the United States by 2030. China is also developing a new generation of stealth drones, called Anjian, or Dark Sword, whose capabilities could surpass those of the U.S.'s fleet. China has 11 drone bases almost completed along its coastline and those drones are almost certain to come into conflict with those Japan purchases from the United States. And that is before we take North Korea's erratic diversions into account.

China's military expenditure therefore is, along with the threat it poses, rising at a phenomenal rate and, although China still lags behind India and the major Western nations in terms of blue water capability, this is not such a hindrance if China can grab and hold choke points essential to her medium-term ambitions. Modern commerce since Adam Smith's time has functioned under the umbrellas of either the British Royal Navy or the U.S. Navy, each of which functioned by controlling the world's major naval choke points. Choke points remain a prominent issue today in the global economy and shipments of goods, particularly oil, and the Chinese Navy's proximity to the Coco Islands, as well as its increasing capacity to dominate the South China Sea through the choke points of the Spratly and Paracel Islands, gives the Middle Kingdom an unprecedented degree of latent leverage to bully its neighbors into submission.

Accelerated Chinese influence in Myanmar is of particular concern to India and other pivotal regional powers as it gives the Chinese the potential to deploy their sea power in India's maritime areas of interest, and to eventually directly threaten India's eastern flank; they already dominate the Himalayas through their colonization of Tibet and their emasculation of the inner states of Nepal and Bhutan, thus giving them a huge strategic advantage in the next trans Himalayan conflict. Developments regarding the establishment of a Chinese electronic listening post in the Coco Islands, just off the northern tip of North Andaman Island, assistance to the Myanmar junta to improve and develop naval ports and facilities on the Arakan coast, also threaten Thailand and the oil supplies of Japan, Korea and Taiwan, the three key American defence spokes in Asia.

China's stated imperialist objectives of the forcible subjugation of Taiwan, and control of the Spratly and Paracel Islands, as well as its intimidation of Vietnam and the Philippines coupled with the military neutralization of Japanese power all run counter to the interests of all other regional powers that refuse to be Chinese vassal states. Although China currently lacks the overt military capability to successfully prevail in any of her main imperialist ambitions, that may not be of import if she can control the relevant choke points over time by stealth or threat.

Although China has so far failed to produce a viable domestic combat aircraft, neither has Israel, South Africa, India, Taiwan, or South Korea, all of whom also import systems from one of the five main military aircraft producers (the U.S.A, Russia, Britain, France, and Germany). This is because the economies of scale required to finance, research, develop, and produce all the systems and sub-systems that make up today's frontline combat aircraft are not available to smaller industrial countries nor to large developing countries with smaller GNPs and smaller industrial bases; this latter point is making Russia lag increasingly behind the West in most areas of military technology. However, because Israel is selling relevant materiel and technology to China and because China is developing Assassin's Mace weaponry, and because the United States and her allies cannot compete in manpower or in staying power, China's shrinking technological military dearth is not decisive.

Nor should China's diplomatic prowess be underestimated. All ten of the anti China proposals to the UN Human Rights Committee over China's violations of human rights failed because China could mobilize her client states to defeat the modest measures. This robust if somewhat underhanded diplomacy indicates that China only really lags the United States in military materiel and not in diplomatic or economic clout.

Although Chinese propagandists often stress the perceived remilitarization of Japan as well as Indian naval, nuclear and missile capabilities, China has only directly attacked Vietnam in recent years. The farcical attacks on Vietnam as well as the Revolution in Military Affairs, as demonstrated by the United States' armed forces victories in the wars of the Yugoslav succession and the more recent Gulf wars, show that China is best biding her time for now.

Though Japan too is biding her time, she is doing so as the Chinese noose slowly and inexorably tightens around her neck. China has an expansionist and exploitative foreign policy which serves into her domestic needs. Japan not only still seems to have no effective autonomous foreign policy but, her emasculated navy apart, no effective means of implementing any such policy. That being so, the book's main lesson that Japan remains a "toothless tiger" not only still holds but is much more obvious now than it was in 2001 before China started her massive military build ups.

Introduction

There is a specter haunting Japan and Asia: the specter of Chinese communism. This specter takes two forms: the overt, military one that her vast defense forces pose and the covert diplomatic one undermining America's key alliance with Japan. The following chapters detail the challenge China poses not only to Taiwan, South Korea, and other regional powers but also against Japan, through its maritime adventurism in the South China Sea, its military skirmishes with Japan's closest allies, and its diplomatic efforts to get the United States to abandon Asia altogether.

There is also a specter haunting China: the specter of national disintegration. This specter also takes two forms: (1) the overt military, economic, and political pressure from Taiwan, Japan, and the United States, which requires China to divert huge resources to try to match their punch, and (2) the internal economic contradictions undermining Beijing's authority, which threaten to unleash social anarchy in Asia's Middle Kingdom.

The first four chapters detail these two threats. They paint a picture of an aggrieved China only now emerging from over a century of foreign dominance as a young and vibrant country determined to take its rightful place at Asia's helm. The military and other threats China's emergence poses to Japan in particular are also detailed, as are Japan's gamut of options.

Japan's leaders must deal with the two opposing threats China poses. On the surface, the balance of military and political power in the region continues to shift toward China and away from Japan and her allies. Eventually, the U.S. Seventh Fleet, which has blocked China's maritime ambitions for the last fifty years, will sail home to Hawaii. When it does, China will eventually incorporate Taiwan and the islands of the South China Sea into her vast kingdom. China's resulting hegemony will put a severe strain on the weakest link in America's Asian defense strategy—Japan, Asia's toothless tiger. This toothless tiger has been in a deep slumber for the last fifty years. It has slept so soundly that North Korea now lobs missiles across her territory with impunity. China, meanwhile, encroaches into Japan's territorial waters on an almost daily basis. All Japan can currently do is toothlessly grin and bear it and hope that things do not get worse.

But life does not stand still. China's military and energy policies are changing the strategic map of Asia and, if Japan and her allies continue to snooze, China will achieve regional hegemony. China's sheer size and vitality will put it on a collision course with the United States. If Japan does not play its part in that confrontation, it will find itself forever marginalized in international affairs. Japan will have to play second fiddle to China.

That is one worrying scenario. Beneath the surface, there is another equally dangerous current forming. If China follows the lead of Indonesia and the former Soviet Union and collapses into anarchy, it will drag Japan and the whole of Asia down as well. Japan must prepare for both contingencies. Japan must not only develop a military presence but must also begin to develop diplomatic skills, which have been sorely lacking over the last fifty years. Japan must strive for some much-needed long-term stability. In all probability, Asia's future will be a mixture of both scenarios, a mixture of chaos and confusion. That being so, Japan's strategy will also have to be a mixture of diplomacy, economic aid, trade, and remilitarization. If Japan is to guarantee its future, it must begin to act on all those fronts now. It must make hard economic, diplomatic, and military decisions.

Although China dominates the first four chapters, it is not the only major actor in the area under discussion. Korea, Japan's closest neighbor, is the most militarized piece of real estate on the planet. And then there is the nuclear tension between Pakistan and India. Russia, Japan's northern neighbor, remains ill at ease with its lost power and lost cohesion. To the south, meanwhile, Indonesia is imploding. Japan cannot stay oblivious to the confusion that surrounds her, or to the resulting chaos, which may engulf her. Japan lives in a volatile region that will only become more volatile with time. Japan must make the appropriate response.

The Cold War era response would have been for Japan to unilaterally rearm, to be able to throw China back into the ocean, should matters ever come to a head. Although this simplistic strategy has its proponents on Capitol Hill, it also has two major downsides, which are respectively covered in Chapters One to Four and Five to Eight. First, irrespective of any moral arguments, a more sophisticated response is needed because China is simply too big to be pushed around. This response has to entail a mixture of the carrot and the stick, without unduly antagonizing China in the process. Even at the height of the Cold War, the Americans pursued a similar path with the Soviets. They built the world's most awe-inspiring defense system, with which they stared down the Soviets during the Cuban Missile Crisis. In the end, however, jaw-jaw not war-war won the Cold War for the United States and her allies. This book shows that the same strategy is needed in Asia.

The second half of the book builds on this point. Quite simply, the second problem with unilateral rearmament is that Japan is in no position to attack anybody in the foreseeable future. That being so, her strategy must be one of defensive remilitarization coupled with a proactive diplomatic strategy. Japan, like any other nation, has inalienable rights, which must be promoted and defended. Although Japan must continue to use its formidable checkbook, it must use more conventional diplomatic and military methods as well. Therein lies Japan's dilemma.

For the first time since 1945, Japan must make hard military and diplomatic choices. Japan must develop a sword and a shield. This book explains not only why Japan must develop the bomb, today's hi-tech sword, but also why she must commit herself to America's controversial Theater Missile Defense (TMD) shield system. However, even Japan's possession of a nuclear deterrent and a fully functional TMD system would not be enough to guarantee the peace that Japan's economy needs. Japan must also play a much more forthright diplomatic role than it has in the past. Japan must, in other words, learn to say more than yes or no. She must speak regularly, she must speak softly, and she must carry a very big stick. This, of course, is contrary to the more orthodox dictum that Japan should forever remain an international weakling and hope against hope that the long-term threats to its national interest disappear. That would be nice—as nice as any other daydream. However, because the Seventh Fleet will eventually abandon Asia, Japan must make the necessary preparations now. The Japanese tiger needs the necessary teeth and claws to fend for itself in tomorrow's Asia. That way, when America withdraws, Japan will be able to speak to its neighbors from a position of mature military strength consistent with its economic strength. It will join the United States and China as one of Asia's premier powers and policemen. And that will benefit everybody, the leaders of North Korea excepted.

Declan Hayes, Tokyo, 2001

The Prospects for War

Japan must bite the bullet—and be prepared to use the bullet as well. Japan must build a credible defense force to underwrite her economic might. When China and North Korea flex their muscles, Tokyo will need sharp fangs to snap back at them. Otherwise, she will become a vassal state.

Tokyo's role as a toothless tiger has already cost her dear. Japan's Northern Territories—the islands of Etorofu, Kunashiri, Shikotan, and Habomai—are now the last and final outpost of European imperial power in Asia; Russia annexed them in September 1945 and has illegally occupied them ever since. Japan has no military leeway to force the issue. All she can do is toothlessly grin and bear it.

While Russia has posed a threat for the last three hundred years in the north, China poses a far more insidious one in the distant south. Only America's bases stand in the way of her eventually reincorporating Okinawa and the surrounding islands and waters into her vast Middle Kingdom. And now these bases are under threat by public opinion and myopic policy makers in Washington.

Although Tokyo has showered the islanders with money to buy

them off, the locals want the bases gone. And Tokyo's checkbook diplomacy has not changed that. Nor has the patchwork PR of the U.S. forces on the island. Sooner or later, the Yanks will be gone. And then there will be a new guy on the block.

That new guy is China, which is gradually reestablishing its primacy in East Asia. China, which has only recently emerged from a Western-induced century of shame, is now reasserting herself in the region. And so far, there is little Japan can do except marvel at the rise to political, economic and military prowess of her giant neighbor. Japan's political paralysis presents its own dangers. Asia's strategic map is changing. And all Japan can do is stare in awe as it changes. This will prove to be an expensive luxury.

Once the Seventh Fleet sails home to Hawaii, the Chinese will fill the resulting political, economic, and military void. This has been the case with the Philippines and Okinawa will be not be any different. Japan will then have to crawl out from under America's security umbrella. Unable to hide any longer behind Uncle Sam's apron strings, Japan will have to bite the bullet. And make them in greater numbers as well! Japan will have to develop a formidable military deterrence to China and other regional powers, North Korea in particular. If not, when America goes, so too will Japan—into the orbit of the Chinese People's Liberation Army. That is the logic of political paralysis.

Japan, which has been a military eunuch for the last sixty years, is now in a bind. If Japan joins the Theater Missile Defense (TMD) program with America, South Korea, and Taiwan, she could become entrapped in a shooting war with China; if she does not join the TMD system, America might abandon her for reasons of economic expediency for China. Japan is in an invidious position. America's Seventh Fleet will, in the final analysis, sail home across the Pacific Ocean. Japan will have to live with the consequences—unless she begins to build the necessary diplomatic and military bridges now.

Japan has been singularly weak in both of these fields. Her

foreign policy has always been extremely simplistic. She has only ever allied herself to one great power at a time. These were, in historical order, Great Britain, Nazi Germany, and the United States. The alliance with Nazi Germany, as well as being a total disaster for Japan, was totally simplistic as it ruled out flexibility, which has, for example, been the hallmark of Britain's international diplomacy for centuries. Japan's alliance with the United States is equally simplistic as it rules out the more flexible approach needed to deal with China and Japan's other neighbors in today's dynamic world. Clearly, Japan needs to hone up her diplomatic skills to deal with today's more fluid times. She also needs to revamp her military capability as an integral part of this process.

The fear of a revived Japanese military capability is in itself a powerful propaganda tool which Beijing and Pyongyang have repeatedly exploited with telling account themselves. Beijing, faced with the threat of internal meltdown, uses the external threat of a revived Japan as an internal unifying force—and as a justification to build a buffer zone in the waters off Okinawa. The removal of U.S. forces from Okinawa will radically alter Asia's political landscape. If the Americans desert Okinawa and Japan does not reassert itself in the region, China will fill the resulting power vacuum. The strategic dilemma for Japan is how to speak quietly to China while developing a sufficiently big stick to use in self-defense.

Japan needs only to look at the Philippines, which closed down American bases at Subic Bay some years ago and now finds the Chinese People's Liberation Army Navy conducting military exercises only a few vulnerable miles from its main islands. And the Philippines has enjoyed a historically more harmonious relationship with China than has Japan.

Currently, only the American bases in Okinawa maintain the political tranquillity of the South China Sea. And even they are no panacea. Roughly 20,000 of the 29,000 troops on Okinawa are Marines attached to the Seventh Fleet and are routinely deployed anywhere in the Seventh Fleet's sprawling operating areas of the

Western Pacific and Indian Oceans. Okinawa is, in other words, merely a convenient parking lot; the fact that it is on Japanese soil is secondary to its main policing mission. These U.S. Marines have nothing to do with the defense of Okinawa, or of the rest of Japan for that matter. Recent revelations of U.S. plans to blast the island and its inhabitants to smithereens in the event of a Soviet attack have not endeared them to the locals, who remember how the Japanese Imperial Army wantonly sacrificed them as literal cannon fodder in their battles against the Americans in 1945. On the positive side, they do show Okinawa's continuing strategic importance. The United States did not want the island falling into the enemies' hands. Cold consolation to the Okinawans but consolation nonetheless. The fact is that Okinawa's strategic position gives it immense value to the United States and her allies, one which the opponents of the American alliance downplay, when they don't totally dismiss it out of hand. Okinawa remains the linchpin of American military power in the Asia-Pacific theater.

Okinawa is America's frontline in the South China Sea. The joint American and Japanese forces stationed there prevent China's navy asserting itself in the South China Sea. Okinawa is the fall back position if America and her allies are ever again pushed off the Korean peninsula. Okinawa is the base from which American reinforcements will be rushed to Taiwan in a doomsday situation. Okinawa is the linchpin of linchpins.

Okinawa keeps the sea lanes open; it preserves the status quo, the Pax Americana which has been so good for Japan. And therein lies the rub. It keeps a non-Asian power, the United States, at the helm of Asia and therefore keeps a major Asian nation, China, down. China is quite understandably peeved at this attempt to corral her. In as much as Japan is party to this arrangement, she is peeved at Japan. And because she is peeved, she may well be prepared to do something to remedy the situation in time. And China has plenty of time.

China sees Okinawa as a paper tiger. The Marine force on

Okinawa is too small for major combat engagements and generally too immobile even for establishing tripwires or slowing down a strong adversary, such as the Chinese People's Liberation Army, in the early phases of a sustained attack. The logic of this interpretation is for the Marines to disengage from Okinawa altogether. Although Okinawa is a convenient parking lot, Marine patrols of the Western Pacific could begin and end from Hawaii or the continental United States instead of Okinawa. China is prepared to wait for the logic of this argument to permeate its way through into official policy.

Although this makes good housekeeping sense in Washington, it spells strategic disaster for Tokyo. Just as America's withdrawal from Subic Bay created a vacuum that China quickly filled, so also will the abandonment of Okinawa create another, bigger vacuum that China will also fill. China's leaders are using nationalistic rhetoric to keep their vast regime together and any diminution of the American forces in Okinawa will only encourage China to increase its war of words.

Because Japan has been as quiet as a mouse for the last fifty years, she is ill equipped to engage in the propaganda wars that will ensue when the Seventh Fleet weighs anchor. She will wake up to find Uncle Sam's Navy gone back to Hawaii and her own neighbors descending into anarchy. And Japan will be helpless to remedy the situation. China is not the only source of concern. Far from it!

Asia is awash with flash points that the United States, Japan and their allies must continue to monitor. These include the four Kurile Islands, occupied by Russia since 1945 and claimed by Japan; North Korea, still isolated, still armed and still extremely dangerous; the Diaoyu/Senkaku Islands subject to rival claims by Japan, China and Taiwan; Taiwan itself, under almost continuous military threat from China; Myanmar, controlled by an oppressive military junta; Cambodia, emerging from decades of strife and mayhem and always facing the prospect of war with Vietnam; the

Spratly Islands, variously claimed by China, the Philippines, Vietnam, Malaysia, Taiwan, and Brunei; Mindanao, where Muslim insurgents continue to undermine the government of the Philippines; East Timor, the former Portuguese territory annexed by Indonesia in 1975 and only now emerging from an Indonesian-inspired genocide campaign; Indonesia itself, Asia's Yugoslavia, the world's most populous Muslim nation, awash with ethnic and sectarian strife; Kashmir, the epicenter of a nuclear roulette game between India and Pakistan; and Bougainville, fighting for independence from Papua New Guinea. And then, of course, there is the mess of Russia, the former "evil empire" that continues to spiral out of control. This is a long and incendiary list, needing only a spark to create mayhem.

These flash points will, sooner or later, blow up into more hot wars. This is all the more so as Asia is strikingly under-institutionalized. Unlike Europe, which is awash with flash points of its own, Asia has no real working equivalents of NATO and the European Union to iron out the area's many differences. Quite the contrary in fact. The end of the Cold War has ignited an arms race in Asia and the diffusion of high-tech military capabilities throughout the region. Therefore, future wars in Asia will be very bloody and very costly to all involved. A more hard-line regime in Vietnam could, for example, decide to formally colonize much of Cambodia. Already, large numbers of Vietnamese civilians are encroaching into Cambodia much the same way as Chinese civilians are colonizing the sparsely populated Russian Far East. Because the Cambodian government is currently friendly with Hanoi, this has not yet caused much bloodshed.

However, conflicts between these two old adversaries will almost certainly call a third player into the ring. That third player is China, which sees Vietnam as a major threat and which desperately wants to break the growing working alliance between Taipei and Hanoi. If India or any of China's other potential enemies decided to join in, the conflict would quickly spread. The same would be true if China were to be drawn into a major war between India and Pakistan.

Russia, India, China, Pakistan, Indonesia and most of Asia's other key players are held together as national entities only by the slimmest of threads. It would not take much to unravel those threads and to thereby set the continent ablaze. Indonesia, East Timor, Kashmir, and Chechnya show the violence the region is capable of. Many such scenarios can be painted and summarily dismissed out of hand. However, we should ignore these underlying currents at our peril. In Indonesia, Malaysia, and to a lesser extent Vietnam, there is a growing anti-Western sentiment arising from the impact of the earlier Asian financial crisis and the U.S.-led invasions and occupations of Iraq and Afghanistan. So, too, has America's refusal to become embroiled in the East Timor peacekeeping operation. It lends credence to the idea that America is disengaging from the region—and that America's refusal to become involved in an Asian ground war has created a vacuum that China, in particular, will eventually fill.

China, Asia's Middle Kingdom, observes all of this. China wants to be the Middle Kingdom of old, to be the center of the region, not the center of a bloody storm. Because she sees the bush fires raging along her borders, she must be prepared to stamp them out. As later chapters explain, she is modernizing her vast army to be able to do just that. China is not going to let these bush fires consume her. She will ruthlessly stamp them out.

Just like China, Japan cannot stay immune from any widening and deepening blood bath on its doorstep either. She too has to defend her vital interests or perish. Japan must therefore beef up her military capability and face the political and military backlash from her neighbors and fair weather allies. Japan must be able to defend the sea-lanes, which are vital to her commerce. If she cannot defend them, she will perish in the political storms that lie ahead.

Japan, unlike Italy and Germany, has spent the last fifty years in the international sin bin, because of its aggressive actions in the Pacific War. But just as times have changed, so also must Japan. Japan must become as politically responsible in Asia as Germany is in Europe. This, needless to say, brings immense risks with it. A rearmed Japan runs the risks of being labeled an aggressive and dangerous Japan. An aggressive and dangerous Japan runs the risk of being annihilated by nuclear weapons. A nuclear attack on Tokyo would obliterate Japan's capacity to function, let alone to wage war. Whereas as few as three nuclear missiles are enough to effectively immobilize Japan, the geographies of Russia, China, and America make them much more elusive nuclear targets. Their populations are not as concentrated as are Japan's. Because of its vulnerability, Japan must be cautious in any further rearmament it undertakes. It must be aware of the retaliatory risks it runs and the power and determination of its potential enemies. But it must rearm.

Japan can no longer be the world's sole military eunuch. Nor can she be the world's last diplomatic mouse. Japan has vital interests that must be protected by the most appropriate means. Japan's voice must be heard in its own backyard.

Asia needs Japan to stabilize it. And Japan needs a stabilized Asia. America can no longer fill that role. Nor can America continue to be the de facto defender of Japan. Japan must stand on her own two feet. She must scrap her outmoded constitution and build a formidable defense force to replace America's over-stretched forces. Allied to that, she must play a leading diplomatic role in Asia commensurate with her economic role. If not, she will pay a price for her silence.

Japan can no longer shelter under the American military and diplomatic umbrella for the simple reason that America's shield will, together with the American sword, eventually be removed from the Asian theater altogether. The United States, which acted as policeman to the world, is no longer able to fill that role in Asia. The United States is simply not equipped to fight more than a handful of regional wars at any one time. The Iraqi Gulf War stretched

America's capabilities to their limits. Iraq, a minnow state, self-sufficient only in dates, oil and tinpot dictators, stretched the American alliance to its limits. To defeat Saddam Hussein, the United States deployed 75 percent of its active tactical aircraft, more than 40 percent of its modern battle tanks, almost 50 percent of its aircraft carriers, nearly 40 percent of its aircraft carriers and almost 50 percent of its marine personnel. The Kosovo conflict put a similar strain on her capabilities. An Asian crisis, coupled with further flare-ups in the Balkans or the Middle East, would stretch the United States to breaking point. Future conflicts, in other words, will need regional inputs. Japan, as America's premier Asian ally, must make the hard and unpalatable choices. Japan must make the commitment. Japan must develop her own military muscle. She will have to flex them in the future.

The balance of power in Asia continues to shift in favor of the big battalions. These include China, Pakistan, India, North Korea, Russia and a host of other unstable countries, which interact with them. It is a heady and potentially lethal brew that will, sooner or later, enmesh Japan. Japan cannot be immune to the growing pains of Asia, China in particular. China, Asia's Middle Kingdom, finds herself jostling for elbowroom with her neighbors. To this end, China uses North Korea as a buffer state, she leans on Taiwan, she occupies Tibet, arms Pakistan, bankrolls Myanmar, clashes with the Philippines and Vietnam over the Spratly Islands, she plays power politics in Cambodia and, poker-faced, she warns Japan and other countries against destabilizing the region. China, the new guy on the block, is rapidly filling many of Asia's military and political vacuums. China's sheer size and rate of economic growth make her an unprecedented force for change in the area. This is true regardless of whether China's nation-building designs are fulfilled or not.

If Beijing's regional tussles were not bad enough, China also runs the risk of implosion and the accompanying anarchy, which characterized the disintegration of the Soviet Union. Although

Beijing has checked the secessionist tendencies of her peripheral areas for the moment, economic growth and increased interaction with the outside world are, however slowly, opening the flood-gates. Because Beijing chooses to see Taipei's hand behind these secessionist movements, she could very well use these as an excuse to attack Taiwan. Japan could not stand idly by and watch Asia's main buffer state fall.

The key question facing Japan and her allies is how to respond to the increasingly assertive Chinese dragon. The only rational policy at the moment is a policy of economic and diplomatic engagement, while continuing military preparations for whatever confrontations may lie ahead. China is growing and Japan will have to decide how it will respond.

That is the primary lesson of China's South Seas policy. Taken together with its activities in Mynanmar, China's gunboat diplomacy over the Spratlys shows its relentless push towards the sea-lanes which skirt the Spratlys and which hold the key to the future of Asia, Okinawa and all of Japan included. China has already come to blows with the Philippines and Vietnam over these tiny islands. China has now lodged her armed forces on many of the islands comprising the archipelago. These include the aptly named Mischief Reef, which is less than 200 kilometers off Palawan, one of the main islands of the Philippines. This is a serious affront to the Philippines, which, unlike Vietnam—and Japan—has traditionally enjoyed amicable relations with Beijing. China's gunboats and a gung-ho Vietnam, in the absence of any meaningful institutional arrangements, ensure that further conflict is inevitable. Because these conflicts must eventually involve Japan, Japan must prepare. Japan must rearm.

China's adventurism also impinges on Indonesia's interests and, by extension, those of Japan as well. Since 1974, Chinese maps have included an exclusive economic zone of 371 kilometers around the Spratly Islands. This, in turn, cuts into part of Indonesia's rich gas field based around Natuna Island. Because this is a direct threat to Exxon's proposed $35 billion deal with Indonesia to develop the gas field, it is also a threat to Japan's long-term energy needs. The Spratly Islands dispute, in other words, presents a multi-faceted challenge to Japan.

The Spratly Islands standoff could erupt at any time and turn the South China Sea into a war-zone. China and Vietnam have already shed blood over these islands. Because none of the other powers occupying the Spratlys is strong enough to stand up to Beijing without outside help, China's claims are particularly destabilizing in this regard. She has clashed with the forces of both Vietnam and the Philippines, she claims territory within gunshot range of the Philippines and she claims large parts of the gas fields north of Indonesia's Natuna Island as her own sovereign territory. Because China cannot be contained even in the South China Sea, Japan must adopt a much more sophisticated approach to dealing with her giant neighbor. Realistically, this approach must involve the carrot and the stick, a judicious balance between jaw-jaw and war-war. Japan's diplomats must drive home to their Chinese counterparts the overall geo-strategic consequences of their actions. China's claims run the very real risk of causing further bloodshed—and the chance of a massive strategic miscalculation with devastating consequence for all involved. Logically, some of that blood will have to be Japanese.

Taiwan, China's "renegade province," has also played an aggressive role in the dispute—and thereby increased the capacity for such a catastrophic miscalculation. She sent a naval mission of armed patrol boats to the Spratly Islands in March 1995 but recalled them before they reached the disputed territories. Taiwan fluctuates between China's policy of turning the South China Sea into a Chinese-dominated lake and Vietnam's policy of thwarting China's maritime imperialism. This is a dangerous game to play and, though Taiwan might not become embroiled in the initial stages of any hot war, she could well be the spark that ends up incinerating all parties to the dispute, Japan included.

Although the PLA's sporadic military aggression in the Taiwan Strait ensures that Taiwan has more pressing security problems of its own, Tokyo must take all of these developments into account. Given recent military build-ups in the region, the Spratly Islands conflict represents a serious challenge to regional stability. Given that a large number of countries lay claim to the islands and that the Spratlys are scattered over a vast sea expanse, they would be very difficult to defend. Only a country with a substantial blue-water navy could hope to control all of the islands. Because China, the power most likely to be able to control them in the long run, is over a decade away from having the required capability, Japan and her allies must now launch their own build-up. Although localized skirmishes between a handful of claimants is a more likely scenario in the shorter term, China's long-term plans demand a careful counter plan of diplomatic and naval engagement to emasculate them. Japan must be at the center of any such plan. Japan must acquire naval claws. She will have to bare them in the future.

The Spratlys is a major regional issue, one that will set precedents for other future flash points. This being so, Japan must be involved, preferably as an honest broker. But for Japan to be involved, she will have to take her head out of the sands and realize that the diplomatic landscape is changing by the day. The Asian tigers are aiming to secure their place in the sun. If Japan wishes to stay at the economic helm of Asia, she will have to engage herself in these disputes. That will involve Japan engaging with China.

China has blown hot and cold on the Spratlys for many years now. Her gunboat diplomacy has been backed up by more moderate calls for the claimants to jointly develop the area. This, most likely, is merely a ploy to divide the other claimants and to institute joint ventures bilaterally with Vietnam, the Philippines, and Malaysia in certain defined areas. Although Japan's fabled checkbook could go a long way to resolving this dispute, such a division of the spoils would not, however, settle the issue.

Crucially in all of this, China claims sovereignty to the entire region and refuses to compromise on that fundamental point. The Spratly archipelago falls within what has been termed China's "nine dotted lines" in the South China Sea. The expression refers to a map concocted by the anti-Communist government of the Republic of China in 1947. The line swings deep into the South China Sea, and the Vietnamese somewhat sarcastically describe it as the "Chinese cow tongue licking up the South China Sea." In Chinese mythology the islands in the South China Sea are correspondingly described as a part of the "tongue of the dragon." This ancient mythology fits into the current Chinese objective of controlling the area's sea-lanes and, by extension, the economies of Japan and the other nations, which depend on those sea-lanes for their vital supplies.

China is working to a logical plan of action whereas Japan is just bumbling through. China's moves are part of a wider campaign to maneuver itself into a position to control shipping from East Asia through the Malacca Strait, which adjoins the Spratly Islands, should circumstances warrant it. The shipments along the sea-lanes flanking the Spratlys account for some US$570 billion a year, or 15 percent of all global cross-border trade. Some 75 percent of Japan's oil is shipped through these sea-lanes. If China subjugates the Spratlys while continuing her alliance with the military dictatorship of Myanmar, she will gain control of Japan's oil flows. She will have the capacity to stop that oil flow on any occasion that suits her.

Currently the U.S. Seventh Fleet keeps these arteries open and the Fifth Fleet performs a similar job in the Persian Gulf. Both of these massive armadas serve the interests of both the United States and Japan. But the Chinese navy does not. It must serve Beijing. It must keep the oil flowing freely to China, even if this is contrary to the interests of Japan. There is, in other words, a risk that Japan's oil tap will be severed in the years ahead. Japan must make efforts now to ensure that this does not happen.

This is not just idle speculation. China is now enraging the

Philippines by extending a fishing ban well into the disputed area in the South China Sea. The Chinese Navy is imposing an annual two-month fishing ban around the Spratly Islands—the Nansha Islands, as they call them. Manila points out the simple fact that the islands are more than 1,000 miles from the Chinese mainland and some 700 miles south of Hainan Island. They are less than 200 miles from the Philippines' mainland. Although The Philippines continues to protest the moves, it lacks the military muscle to deter China. Manila sees the Chinese dragon moving southwards, devouring all before it, unimpeded.

The view from China is naturally enough very different. They merely see it as an attempt to protect their vital sea routes. Just like Japan and the United States, China has to ensure that her supplies of oil continue to arrive unimpeded. And just like Washington, Beijing is deploying her navy to ensure that the black gold continues to arrive to her shores. The fact that this policy poses a threat to Japan is not Beijing's primary concern. They have the much more daunting task of keeping their vast nation afloat. For that overriding purpose, they need a strong navy to guarantee their oil and a steely determination to defend and promote their national objectives.

As part of this process, the Beijing authorities argue that they must be strong on the Spratlys, on the Japanese-controlled Senkaku Islands and on other matters concerning Chinese sovereignty, to stop Taipei using these issues to undermine them. This is cold comfort to Manila, which sees China imposing fishing bans on her doorstep. Where fishing bans lead, limits to traditional freedom of navigation will follow. Japan, in other words, could, in the fullness of time, find herself blocked from using the sea-lanes of the South China Sea. Japan, in such a scenario, will be crippled, isolated and devoid of oil and its other key imports. It will be reduced to being a tributary of Greater China. Because China's vast oil needs might make the tribute exorbitantly debilitating with time, Japan must prepare.

The question of American disengagement from Okinawa therefore is a multilayered question. It is as much about China's future power projections as it is about the Pentagon's bookkeeping. Japan must take these realities into account when formulating its own policy towards the Kuriles, the Spratlys, the Senkaku Islands and in other potential areas of conflict with China and Russia. Japan, for example, has the choice of independent deterrence; it could call attention to the Kuriles by frustrating Russia's nuclear fleet. Japan's navy could, for example, block Russia's four straits of access to the open Pacific. Whether Japan could deal with Russia's probable over-reaction to any such move would determine in large part the efficacy of Japan's strategy. Given that China would capitalize upon any unilateral move by Japan, Japan would have to be very careful in adopting such a provocative stance. Japan needs all the friends she can muster. The problem is that Asia's turbulent waters make it difficult to differentiate current friend from future foe.

Because Russia is the weak link in the chain, Japan must build financial bridges with Moscow, whose far east is over-exposed to China's demographic and economic pressures. Indeed, only Japanese financial support, including orders for military hardware, can keep the Russian Far East out of Beijing's grasp. Moscow, in other words, does not present the primary threat. Recent joint military maneuvers between the two neighbors have reduced the risks on Japan's northern borders even further.

These friendly visits aside, there can be no real rapprochement until Russia returns the four islands north of Hokkaido their military continue to occupy. Despite this ongoing insult to her national pride, Japan is doing all she can to build friendly relations with Russia. Japan is one of the key countries that still lend Russia the vast sums of money it needs to keep afloat. If Japan's checkbook diplomacy is to work anywhere, it must be with cash-strapped Russia. Other security problems cannot be so easily ameliorated.

China and North Korea are, far and away, Tokyo's two most urgent sources of concern. Both have the substantial domestic arms industries needed to perpetrate war. Both countries, for their own strategic reasons, are exporting their Silkworms and Rodong missiles to the world's trouble spots, the rogue nations of the Middle East in particular. All of this means that Japan will have to look at a canvas slighter wider than Japan and its surrounding waters. China's alliances with the rogue Middle Eastern nations and its increased presence in the South China Sea puts China at an immense strategic advantage. She could end up being able to cut off oil supplies to Taiwan, South Korea, and Japan—if the situation warranted it. Japan, to survive, would have to call on the United States to assist. Alternatively, she would have to have the autonomous capability to resist. She would need her own teeth, her own formidable fighting forces to resist the world's largest army, the Chinese People's Liberation Army.

Japan must therefore ensure she is in a position to respond by the most appropriate means. This means strengthening her alliances with potential regional allies, building up a blue water navy and being diplomatically prominent throughout the entire Asian arena. All of these are within Japan's capabilities.

Japan must build more local defense alliances. Although Japan has some bitter historical relationships with North East Asia, she has much better ones with South East Asia, where she expelled the Dutch imperial army from Indonesia. Tokyo is also the world's major donor to Cambodia and she can use that as a bargaining lever in the future. Tokyo has also close historical ties with Burma, where China is now particularly active, as well as with Thailand and Vietnam. Although these two latter countries are vital satellite players in the Asian arena, they will need Japanese financial and diplomatic backing to remain independent of Beijing and other regional power brokers.

Thailand is developing its own blue water navy with a power projection capability, not only within her existing territorial waters, but in the Andaman Sea as well. Japan should aid her in this regard, in as much as it checks China's adventurism in Myanmar. Although

Thailand continues to dispute its maritime borders with Burma, Cambodia, and Vietnam, Myanmar is in no position to pressurize Thailand without China's assistance. Cambodia is in no position to threaten anybody and if Japan brokers an alliance between Vietnam and Thailand, the threats of strategic miscalculation in the region will be much reduced.

Although Thailand could also come into conflict with either Indonesia or Malaysia, such contingencies are less likely now than in the past. Even though both Indonesia and Malaysia have increased their military capabilities substantially in recent years, it is doubtful that either will try to project their power far beyond their own waters. Malaysia has toned down its recent vitriolic rhetoric against Singapore, which, in turn, has strengthened its ties with the U.S. Navy by offering it berthing facilities. Although Kuala Lumpur has recently invested in Russian MiG-29s and two British frigates, her leaders will most likely concentrate on reconstruction instead of substantial rearmament. Internal ethnic divisions will, in any event, put a brake on any expansionist plans Malaysia may harbor. Although Jakarta recently purchased British Hawk aircraft and a sizable chunk of the ex-East German navy, her forces are not a credible fighting body. The same is not true of China.

China's sheer size and geographic reach are, in themselves, destabilizing to the current status quo. China's links with Myanmar, for example, opens up another strategic Pandora's box. China is pressing for Myanmar to allow it into Victoria Point, which adjoins the strategic Straits of Malacca. This is the epitome of the PLA's relentless push towards the sea-lanes. This is today's great game, today's equivalent of the imperial rivalries which dominated strategic thinking at the end of the nineteenth century. China's objective of controlling the narrow Straits of Malacca is to control the sea-lanes into and out of Asia. China needs to control these sea routes to guarantee her own oil supplies. Although that is understandable, it comes at a cost to Japan. Japan could, at some future time, find China cutting off her imports. Japan must become engaged now to avoid that calamity.

Today's great Asian game is over energy, oil in particular. East Asia is particularly short of this commodity. Even if we include Indonesia and Vietnam, the Asia Pacific region has less than a tenth of the world's oil. The ratio of reserves to production is only 18 years as compared to 104 years in the Middle East. Because this resource is relatively scarce and vital, energy is one of the main keys to Asia's future. And if China holds the key—or the Straits of Malacca—she will control Asia's future. Asia's energy demands have risen by over 20 percent in a generation. Asia's growing energy demands put increased reliance on the Middle East, the world's cheapest producer. China's $4.5 billion arms deal with Iran signifies the increasing military and economic ties flowing from this new situation. To secure her own oil supplies, China arms the rogue nations of the world—and puts the supplies of Japan and the other law-abiding nations at risk. China's military and economic strategies all combine to form that same conclusion. The sheer size of China's orders has a potential to destabilize the entire region.

China would argue that it is only copying the European and Americans, who have crippled Iraq and who play pipeline politics in the Caucasus to guarantee their own oil supplies. China sees no difference between their policies and actions and her own. And it is difficult to argue with her logic. Oil tankers through the Straits of Malacca are likely to triple as China's economy takes off. China, quite naturally, must protect these lanes. If China, working through Myanmar, secures the Straits of Malacca and turns the South China Sea into a Chinese-controlled lake, American hegemony will be broken. Japanese, Taiwanese, and South Korean oil supplies will effectively be at the mercy of Beijing. A substantial portion of world commerce—primarily the portion on which Japan depends—will be under Chinese, not American, control. They will certainly not be under Japanese control. Japan, however, would have to live with the consequences.

China is guaranteeing her own supply of the black gold. To accomplish that aim, she is transforming the strategic map of Asia out of all recognition. China's oil imports have increased from a mere 3 million tons of crude oil in 1994 to over 25 million tons today. It should surpass 50 million tons in the next few years. Though gigantic, this will be less than a third of its needs. China wants a strategic oil-supply security system, that is, a diverse and safe supply of oil, immune to blockade or American-inspired embargo. To this end, China must build up her navy and her alliances with key satellite states, such as Myanmar. China is involved in a great strategic game that she cannot afford to lose. Although the Chinese are playing out this strategy on a global canvas, it is their alliances and investments in the Middle East and Central Asia that give most cause for concern. Kazakhstan is China's natural bridge to the lucrative Iranian and Iraqi fields. Such a link-up would entrench China's standing as a world power. It would also cripple U.S. efforts to secure the Caspian Sea's oil for the West. China also wants to secure Central Asia's economic cooperation to help pacify Xinjiang, where the Muslim Uighurs are once again getting restless. About 200,000 Uighurs live in Kazakhstan and opposition groups have their bases in Almata, its largest city. China hopes to neutralize this internal threat by its oil diplomacy in Kazakhstan, and its arms diplomacy in Pakistan, Iran, and Iraq.

China is a giant and must think and move like a giant. She is, by far, the biggest and most important of all the Asian tigers. To achieve sustained economic lift-off, she must think and plan and act on a global, gargantuan scale. In the process, she will have to stand on a few toes, Japan's included. The sheer size of China's energy plans makes it a big threat in its own right. China needs to bring on more energy supplies in bigger volumes and at faster rates than any other country in the world has ever attempted. Instead of buying oil on the world's markets, Beijing is buying entire oil fields and shipping the crude back home. China's $50 billion plus investments underscore its determination. It is paying premium price and building strategic pipeline networks crisscross-ing Central Asia. Recently, they have bought estimated reserves of 100 million tons in Venezuela, 200 million tons in Kazakhstan, and 100 million tons in Sudan. They have also struck major deals in Peru, Africa, Turkmenistan, India and the Bashkir Autonomous Republic in Russia. Because the sheer size of China's plans is unprecedented, they will decisively tilt the regional balance of power toward China and away from Japan. There is no peaceful way that China's rise to power can be halted. Her demographics alone see to that.

Although they are acting globally, Beijing are also thinking more locally. China is playing pipeline poker with Russia and the other local powers. Russia sees China's pipelines creating economic vassal states of former Soviet republics such as Kazakhstan—China, incidentally if unsurprisingly, claims oil-rich Kazakhstan as an integral part of its territory. Compounding the game are Beijing's plans to pipe Siberian oil to China and later to Korea and Japan. Iran is developing the pipeline along with China to get a stranglehold on oil from Central Asia. If Iran and China manage to control the flow of oil from the region, the United States will lose control not only of the Caspian Sea but of the Persian Gulf's vast and vital oil supplies to China as well. This would hurt Japan more than most nations. Because this would mean that China would control the supply of oil to Japan, Japan could, at some future stage, find herself being subservient to China, Beijing's vassal state, in other words.

China could therefore become Asia's new dynamo and, in the process, undermine Japan's neo-mercantilist strategy of being an export machine underwritten by the U.S. Seventh Fleet. That is one worrying scenario. There is another.

These pipelines could remain pipedreams. The large funding costs and the fact that they cross some of the world's most inhos-pitable terrain mean that the entire project could collapse and bankrupt China in the process. The same applies to China's Tarim basin oil reserves. They are comprised of less than 30 million tons and are situated in some of the most inhospitable areas not only in China but in the entire world. China just does not have the managerial expertise to bring the Tarim basin project on-stream let alone to man these big overseas operations. Still, this does not get Japan out of the woods by any means. Because China's economic collapse would throw the entire continent into chaos, Japan must watch China's energy moves closely. They pose the polar threats of China assuming regional hegemony or China collapsing into the destabilizing anarchy that characterizes the former Soviet Union. Either scenario brings risks galore for Japan. China is simply too big to be ignored.

China's missiles are also changing Asia's military map; they end America's capacity to militarily dominate Asia's vast geography with its small, dispersed pockets of marine forces. America will eventually have to abandon its Asian bases. Its forward deployment policy will be at an end. Its bases will be too vulnerable. Without forward bases in Asia, there can be no concentration of American military power: weapons cannot even be stored, let alone massed for use. The vulnerability of bases to Chinese missiles is America's singular military weakness in Asia. America's powerful Seventh Fleet cannot make up for the loss of Asian land bases. The Seventh Fleet cannot generate anything like the military power or psychological effect of fixed bases. The most important of these forward bases are those in Japan. Guam, like mainland America, is simply too far away to fill this role. Okinawa is the pivotal, preferred spot. And China's missiles are gradually making those bases redundant to America's strategic thinkers.

But, leaving the very real threat of Chinese missiles aside for the moment, the balance of power even around Okinawa itself is changing. During the 1980s, when the United States stationed 72 F-15 fighters on Okinawa, they were invincible. China's J-6 series, the Mig-19s, were certainly no match for them. Now, however, Washington has scaled back the number of F-15s based in Okinawa to 54. Beijing, meanwhile, has ordered 72 Su-27 "Flanker" fighters from Russia. Because this aircraft can match the capabilities of the F-15, it is only a question of time before Beijing reverses the airpower equation in the East China Sea. Although Washington can always reinforce its Okinawa base, or utilize the F-14s of the U.S. Seventh Fleet or, indeed, call on Taiwan's F-16s or Japan's F-15s for assistance, the impetus is with China. They are increasing their punch while America retreats to Guam and Hawaii. Eventually, Beijing will be strong enough to challenge American might in the seas around Okinawa and the outlying islands they claim. China's air force, of course, will not be its only card. Its formidable missile capability will be a more important psychological force in wresting Okinawa and the surrounding seas and islands away from the West.

China's ballistic missiles already have the capacity to obliterate America's bases in South Korea and Okinawa. America would find it nearly impossible to engage in military operations where Chinese warheads were raining down on Okinawa, causing havoc to American men and materiel. At the very least, it would mean Washington reversing its policy of reducing, if not totally eliminating, American casualties. And if incoming Chinese or North Korean missiles contained atomic, chemical, or biological weapons, as they almost certainly would, the American forward engagement policy would be in tatters. Because neither China nor North Korea will renounce their atomic, chemical or biological options, theater missile defense, incorporating Japan, Korea and the "renegade province" of Taiwan becomes imperative if America is to honor its commitment to stay in Asia. Japan, again, will have to be at the forefront of this development. The explicit and implicit threats missiles hold to American forces in Japan will have to make Japan revitalize not just its response to TMD, but its entire defense strategy as well. Japan will not only have to build a TMD shield; if she wants to deal with China and North Korea as an equal, she will have to have a nuclear-tipped sword as well.

America, for a variety of very sound reasons, will not agree to this. Because of this unchecked threat from ballistic missiles, America's superpower strategy in Asia currently hinges on arms control. However, because arms control treaties perpetuate America's military advantage in Asia, China will never meekly sign on the dotted line and thereby accept her permanent subservience to the United States. Japan will have to prepare for when China finally wields the sword. Currently, Japan must keep its sword sheathed and America's superior regional firepower makes this policy acceptable to Tokyo. However, because it guarantees American regional hegemony, it is not acceptable to Beijing, who must either accept another century of American induced shame or beef up its own defense potential. Missiles provide both the answer to China's dilemma and the source of Japan's.

Because missiles are at the heart of both China's Taiwanese policy and North Korea's fratricidal policy against South Korea, arms-control agreements must concentrate on them and negate the threat they pose. Without the bases, America's forward-engagement strategy will be in tatters. China, however, will not agree to any culling of its missile arsenal, if such a pruning would permanently entrench America's armed forces into the region. Because these hostile missiles are changing the military equation throughout Asia, the problem of missile control is fundamental not only to the immediate defense of Okinawa but to the entire region's future. Okinawa, as the rivalry between Pakistan and India exemplifies, is not the only flash point, where missiles are crucial. Both India and Pakistan have now long-range missiles and nuclear capabilities, bringing lethal dimensions to their old antagonisms. And China and India can now lob missiles at each other over the Himalayas. China also threatens India indirectly by boosting Pakistan's missile force capabilities. All of this is relevant to Japan, which could hardly ignore such major conflagrations on its doorstep.

Japan's neighbors, China, North Korea, India, and Pakistan included, are beefing up their missile capability. As things currently stand, sooner or later, one or more of them will start a war that will drag in others. Japan will not escape unscathed. Because China's missiles could blast Tokyo into eternity within fifteen minutes, Japan must radically rethink its strategy. Japan, influenced by Zen Buddhism and a thousand other debilitating belief systems, has tended to be a slow thinker and an even slower strategic mover. Because it must now be prepared for instant obliteration, it needs to be able to respond quicker to threats on its doorstep. If Japan wants to control her own destiny, Japan must unilaterally rearm.

Japan has been a rather ambivalent member of the Asian community, much as Britain has been a member of the European community. However, Britain's formidable navy gave Britain her autonomy from the days of the Spanish Armada to today. Britain was also a major player in the North Atlantic Treaty Organization (NATO) and she has a major defense industry. This has not been the case with Japan, which has been a military eunuch for a half-century and a diplomatic one since the time of the Meiji Restoration.

Nor can Japan unilaterally depend on America's defense shield. Missile defense will work only if the threat is somehow limited. But there is no cooperative engagement between the United States and the major Asian powers on missiles. Neither China nor India is a party to missile reduction programs. China, to reiterate, can never accept any treaty that perpetuates the invulnerability of U.S. bases in Asia. Nor, for different reasons, can North Korea. The one-sided character of such an agreement—which would permanently lock China and her allies into technological military inferiority to America—guarantees this.

Although Japan has the capacity to alter this equation, China has it well within her capacity to confound America's best missile defenses. China, for example, can frustrate American missile defenses with cheap offsetting actions. Chinese engineers can get their missiles to fly faster, for example, thus forcing America and Japan to go to the massive expense of retrofitting their entire defense force in response. China can also make her missiles spiral in unpredictable paths, which would be next to impossible for defending missiles to hit. China could allow some of her missiles to carry decoys to distract America's defensive missiles. Although counters to these tactics and their numerous variations exist, each solitary change would pump up the defender's costs much further than it does the attacker's. A faster warhead with a smaller chance of detection by radar, for example, necessitates new radars and space-tracking systems to spot it and instantly destroy it. Because it is easier to modify a handful of missiles than it is to change an entire defense system, the advantage is overwhelmingly with the attacker, China in this hypothetical case, and against the defender, American forces in Japan in this case.

In addition to ballistic missiles, advances in cruise missiles, sea mines, and satellite reconnaissance all work against America maintaining its foothold in Asia. Cruise missiles are accurate and inexpensive, and can be armed with nuclear, chemical, or biological warheads. Because their sea-skimming trajectories make them hard to find until it is too late to take evasive action, they are useful for attacking ships. Sea mines in the Straits of Malacca, or the Straits of Taiwan for that matter, would also be particularly debilitating. China is a major producer and exporter of both sea mines and Silkworm cruise missiles. North Korea's navy, as the next chapter shows, has such scenarios at the heart of their own apocalyptic battle plans.

Okinawa's American bases, then, are the most vital lines in the sand thwarting China's ambitions. Even if the American forces remain there, Chinese advances will continue to put them on the defensive. Japan, in revitalizing its own forces, must keep the changing forces of these neighboring powers in mind. In particular, Japan must keep the unstable situation in the Korean peninsula firmly to the forefront of any strategic calculation.

The Dagger to the Heart: KOREA

Korea was the launch pad for two aborted attempts by the Mogul warlord, Kublai Khan, to invade and subjugate Japan late in the thirteenth century. Japan has been wary about Korea ever since. Soon after Itó Hirobumi labeled Korea a "dagger pointing to the heart of Japan" in the nineteenth century, Japan occupied Korea and later annexed it in 1910. The potential threat Korea posed was removed by brutally subjugating it. Although Japan's colonial actions were in accord with European and American norms of the day, the price Japan paid for this bloody conquest includes the ongoing enmity, which still poisons relations between the two countries.

Because North Korea and China seldom let Tokyo forget its past perfidies for long, Japan must always monitor the Korean peninsula very closely. Today, the uncertainties of the Korean Peninsula directly threaten Japan's vital interests. Now that the option of military occupation is no longer viable, Japan must ensure that China, for its own self-protection, does not fill any voids or vacuums Korean unification might bring in its wake. If China dominated the Korean peninsula, the knife at Japan's heart could be easily plunged into her heart. China could use its position to weaken its only serious regional rival. Japan must rearm to protect itself against an emerging united Korea hostile to Japanese interests.

There are more than one million men under arms on the Korean peninsula—more armed soldiers than either the United States or the former Soviet Union maintains. There are over 4 million men mobilized in the four states surrounding Japan—Taiwan, China and the two Koreas. Vladivostock, Russia's military headquarters in the Far East, is only fifty miles away from North Korea! The resulting geostrategic rivalries make Korea the most militarized place on the earth. The strategic uncertainties these giant armies present have haunted the Korean peninsula for the last hundred years. North Korea became an area of strategic interest to tsarist Russia with the completion of the Trans-Siberian railway in the late 19th century. Russia has been trying to influence Korea's destiny ever since, beginning with a treaty in 1884 aimed at the formation of a pro-Russian Korean government to balance growing Chinese and Japanese influence in the peninsula. Japan defeated Russia in a war in 1904, eclipsing Moscow's influence in the peninsula for 40 years, but after the Second World War northern Korea above the 38th parallel was "assigned" to the victorious Soviet Union. Moscow never set up a formal occupation administration in Pyongyang, backing instead Kim Il-sung as leader of a communist government.

After the Korean War, which left the country divided along the 38th parallel, North Korea played off its ideological allies, China and the Soviet Union, against each other. However, when then Soviet leader, Mikhail Gorbachev, in the dying days of Soviet power in 1990 established relations with South Korea and withdrew its aid from Northern Korea, the friendship between Moscow and Pyongyang cooled considerably. Russian President Vladimir Putin visited North Korea in summer 2000, in part to reestablish Russian influence in the peninsula. The visit also had the aim of undermining U.S. plans for an anti-missile shield in the Asia Pacific region. The visit, the first to any part of Korea by a Russian leader, drew Russia back into a pivotal role on the peninsula after a decade of mutual distrust with Pyongyang following the collapse of the Soviet Union.

The most intriguing questions arising from his initiative is how it will affect Washington's long-term plan to erect an anti-missile shield in the Asia Pacific region. This plan is strongly opposed by China and North Korea, and, most likely, Russia as well. Having lost the Cold War in the West, Russia does not want to lose it in the East as well. There is, in other words, a distinct possibility that either Russia or China will continue to prop up North Korea's formidable military machine for their own strategic reasons.

There are simply too many big guys on the Korean block to believe that we will have peace in our time there. Korea remains a giant dagger poised at Japan's exposed heart. The American presence merely ensures that the dagger remains sheathed for the moment. Although the Korean standoff is a residue of the Cold War, several factors make it more mercurial than the European front. The European Cold War had two large and disciplined forces pitted in organized opposition to each other. These two forces— the Warsaw Pact countries and the NATO allies—were respectively anchored around the large and disciplined forces of the Soviet Union and the United States.

Unlike the former Soviet Union, North Korea is not a stable entity in any form or sense. Because it is unstable and uniquely irrational in its foreign affairs, North Korea will not meekly implode as the Soviet Union did. And The People's Republic of China, one of the two main powers behind the Pyongyang throne, is driven by less tractable forces than the former Soviet Union. Taken together, these two regimes make a solution less likely and further friction more likely. Japan must be diplomatically and militarily prepared for whatever emerges from this very unpredictable quarter.

Pyongyang has been part of a power play between China and Russia for the last sixty years. From the end of the Korean War to the end of the Cold War, China and the Soviet Union between them underwrote the North Korean dictatorship. Not even the collapse of the Soviet empire spelt the end of Russian assistance to the Pyongyang regime. Instead of abandoning the Pyongyang regime altogether, Moscow is once again stressing its military treaty obligations with Pyongyang.

Part of the reason for this is that Moscow realizes that Beijing will fill any resulting void. Pyongyang has been more than eager to encourage Beijing in this regard. Pyongyang, almost alone in the international community, supported Beijing's bloody response to the 1989 Tiananmen Square pro-democracy protests. Although China's growing economic relations with South Korea have not adversely affected its relations with North Korea, the main point to note is that Beijing and Moscow continue to underwrite the Pyongyang regime. Tokyo must take all of this into account when formulating an appropriate response. As it reassesses its options, Japan must take these issues of real politik into account.

The Korean problem is much more intractable than most of the world's other regional disputes. Although North and South Korea have been in dispute for over four decades, their confrontation is fundamentally different from the Russo-Chinese confrontation. Whereas the national goals of both China and Russia have not included the utter and ultimate destruction of the other, the two Koreas have been hell-bent on eliminating each other. Particularly noteworthy in this regard is the fact that the North's strategy is still designed to unify—or eliminate—the South by force. North Korea is still pumping large sums of money not only into its military but also into undermining the social stability of the South. Those factors make the possibilities of peaceful coexistence remote. To phrase that another way, peaceful coexistence will remain a pipedream until the regime in Pyongyang is removed. The South's Sunshine policy of economic cooperation notwithstanding, the

Pyongyang regime is unlikely to go quietly. This is particularly so as North Korea further develops its own nuclear deterrence program with the overt and covert support of the Chinese government and job-hunting Russian technicians.

Thus, although North Korea was a pawn—a particularly obnoxious one, but a pawn nonetheless—in the Cold War game, she has now developed her own sets of objectives and strategies and the means to effect them. These means are mostly military and involve an impressive array of nuclear, chemical and biological weapons. The Korean question for Japan therefore becomes a question of how to destroy the Pyongyang regime and achieve the peaceful unification of Korea, while enjoying good relations with the emerging regime and ensuring it remains a buffer between itself and China.

Given the powerful forces involved in the conflict, this is not an easy task! Three major nuclear powers—Russia, the United States, and China—are operative on or adjacent to the Korean peninsula. North Korea, South Korea, Taiwan, and Japan could all develop credible nuclear capability very quickly if they wanted to. Although this atomic anarchy is worrisome, the most immediate and unpredictable threat comes from North Korea, which almost certainly already possesses the nuclear card. North Korea, with a population of only 24 million, has in excess of one million soldiers, the fifth largest standing army in the world after China, the United States, Russia, and India. South Korea is in sixth place with 660,000 soldiers, followed by Pakistan and Vietnam. Because all of these countries are major players in Japan's Asian backyard, Japan must take appropriate action to ensure that it is not the loser in the future conflicts which are inevitable between these large forces. This is all the more so because of the traditional enmity between Japan and Korea, which China would be tempted to exploit for her own strategic ends. Japan has therefore some hard strategic planning ahead of it.

Japan's strategic problems are compounded by North Korea's

apparent irrationality. Despite its now almost perennial state of near famine, North Korea is pouring vast resources into buying and developing missiles and other weapons of mass destruction. North Korea can fulfill its oft-repeated promises to turn Seoul into a sea of fire at any time. North Korea's leaders have little to lose by incinerating Seoul. They certainly have the potential—and the malevolence—to do it. As long as they thought their regime could survive the backlash such an outrage would unleash, they would be reckless enough to launch Armageddon.

Despite the summits in 2000 and 2007 between the leaders of North and South Korea and despite North Korea's establishment of diplomatic relations with Italy, Australia and a handful of other Western countries, this remains an immutable fact. It is nice that the leaders of North and South Korea hold each other's hands when they are together. A unified Korean team marched out together in the opening ceremonies of the 2000, 2004, 2008, and 2012 Olympics, but the two national teams competed separately. It is also nice that a sense of euphoria is sweeping South Korea and that t-shirts showing cartoon pictures of the two Korean leaders toasting each other with champagne, with the slogan "Bottoms Up!" written above, are selling well. It is also nice to know that the tinted sunglasses favored by the North Korean leader have become a popular fashion accessory in the South.

However, the Pyongyang summit was an orchestrated event. Until demilitarization begins, we have to remain ultra-cautious about the North. They may have changed their looks, their smiles, but they have not changed their intentions. The threat from the North—its nuclear and missile program and its huge army are still massed on the border with the south—has not disappeared. The thaw has begun—the hope now is that the smiles and words of goodwill will be translated into action to reduce the tension and fear still palpable on the Korean peninsula.

When Kim Il-sung died in July 1994, North Koreans had never known anything else but his iron rule. The Great Leader, as he styled himself, had shaped and dominated their political and economic affairs for almost half a century. The outpouring of grief was extraordinary: a product of decades of exposure to a grotesque cult of personality. Indeed such has been the isolation of this tiny country that it may be many years before North Koreans realize the true legacy of the Kim Il-sung years, and how far and how fast their fortunes have fallen. The country's fundamental economic difficulties, its inability to feed itself and its internal political contradictions imply it is no longer a question of if the regime collapses but when. However, a rapid disintegration could have a number of dangers for North Korea's neighbors and for the U.S. which maintains a huge military presence in the South. A tidal wave of refugees could flood across the borders into South Korea, Russia and China. Hard-line elements could launch a desperate attack on the South. This nightmare scenario could be triggered by an internal coup by disaffected groups in the military or government. The collapse of the North could lead to a serious escalation of tension between China and the United States. There are, in other words, very many unsolved imponderables.

Pyongyang's ability to launch a sudden, devastating strike against the south as well as missile attacks against Japan and potentially, the United States, remain intact. The North's continuing military buildup close to the Demilitarized Zone (DMZ) means the South and its allies can ill afford to relax. In a statement as as March 2000 to the U.S. Senate Armed Services Committee, the commander of the United States forces in South Korea, General Thomas A. Schwartz, described North Korea as the country most likely to involve the United States in a large-scale war. He said that despite the North's economic hardships, the country's military continued to grow, not only in terms of conventional forces but also increasingly in asymmetrical capability, including missiles and weapons of mass destruction. Although the North says it has suspended its development of new ballistic missiles since September 1999, the U.S. continues to cite the future possibility of a North

Korean missile attack as one of the main justifications for developing anti-ballistic missile defense systems despite the objections of Russia and China. Of particular concern to Washington is an untested North Korean missile, the Taepodong 2, which could reach the western fringes of the U.S. The Taepodong 1 tested by North Korea in 1998 demonstrated the country's ability to strike Japan, as did further tests in 2006, 2009, and 2013.

General Schwartz said that 70 percent of North Korea's active forces, comprising 700,000 troops, 8,000 artillery systems and 2,000 tanks, are still deployed within 100 miles of the DMZ and could attack with minimal preparation. He said that in the previous twelve months, North Korea had done more to improve its military readiness than in the last five years combined, including what he called an ambitious program to improve its ground forces capabilities. Even though North Korea has made the development of its armed forces a top priority in spite of the economic crisis, it is almost impossible to know how effective the country's military capability really is. The unknowns, in other words, continue to outweigh the knowns in intelligence assessments of North Korea.

The Sunshine policy must take those harsh imponderables into account. The reform or even the recovery of North Korea is impossible without cutting its bloated army down to size, without dismantling its armed forces, its trump card, in other words. The army eats up 25 percent of the nation's estimated $22 billion GDP—second in proportionate terms only to Serbia, itself a very bizarre case. Although South Korea spends a more modest 4 percent on her defense needs, this is, in absolute terms, higher than any NATO country, excepting Greece and Turkey which are, in any event, in a state of perpetual near-war with each other. The Korean peninsula is, in other words, comparable only to the most violent places in the world. And this is Japan's backyard, the dagger at her open heart.

Although Korea may be the dagger at Japan's heart, North Korea has gone beyond brandishing mere daggers. Now she brandishes missiles with lethal payloads of mass destruction attached to them. North Korea is the world's largest supplier of ballistic missiles, equipment and technology to Iran, Syria, Egypt, and Pakistan. For North Korea to maintain those markets, she must continue to test-fire them at her own potential enemies. Top of any list of potential enemies stands Japan, emasculated by her own outdated constitution. North Korea's Rodong 1 Missile can carry chemical and biological weapons (CBW) warheads. Osaka is within its range. The Rodong 2 will put Tokyo within range. The Taepo Dong 1 and 2, which she is developing with Iran and China, will make all of Japan vulnerable. Japan must act to remove these hi-tech daggers North Korea brandishes at her. She needs more than a checkbook to defend herself. She needs a stronger TMD system and a stronger army to remove this threat.

Three politically marginalized countries, China, North Korea, and Iran, believe they have a right to develop weapons of mass destruction and strategic conquest while at the same time contending that their potential targets, which include Japan and Taiwan, should not avail themselves of appropriate defense measures. North Korea has actually test-fired her missiles over Japan. These actions not only won North Korea valuable customers from the world's rogue nations but also impressed on Japan the need to be able to defend herself against such irresponsibly risky actions.

North Korea's missile tests over Japan in August 1998, together with her ongoing provocative use of submarines to probe the defenses of Japan and South Korea, must make Japan consider a more proactive defense strategy even if Beijing stands opposed to any signs of Japanese rearmament. Although Japan has lodged strong protests with Pyongyang, such actions are, most likely, a great source of amusement to Pyongyang's dour leaders. Given that they have not backed down from facing the forces of the United States in the last 50 years, it is highly unlikely that Japan's empty rhetoric will cow her. North Korea is a unique case. And because she is unique, she cannot be dealt with by ritual communiqués

and diplomatic shibboleths. The fact that Japan does not appreci-
ate this is worrying. Perhaps a few more North Korean missiles
are needed to wake Tokyo up. If so, North Korea would almost
certainly oblige. The trouble is that North Korea's missiles carry
deadlier payloads than Japan's hollow words.

The same goes for the threats of the United States and South
Korean defense chiefs to use "all available means" against North
Korea if it test-fires any new missiles. North Korea can always test
them in Iranian territory. The bluster of South Korea, Japan and
the United States merely helps North Korea's leaders keep their
people on a tight leash. They also keep in check South Korea's
desire to expand its own missile industry to counter Pyongyang's
threat. Seoul cannot develop its weapon defenses without the
approval of the United States, which wants to avoid a regional
arms race it cannot control. Although Seoul wants to develop a
missile with a range of up to 300 kilometers, prior agreements bar
South Korea from developing missiles with ranges longer than
180 kilometers. This gives a clear advantage to Pyongyang, which
has no such lines in the stratosphere stopping its missile capability. The bottom line of all this is that the advantage lies with North
Korea. Bizarre as it sounds, South Korea and Japan are both on
the defensive against a country where famine is rampant.

North Korea is a case of war being politics by other means. This
is because her collapsed economy affords her no other choices. To
command leverage on the local and world political stages, she
must wave the biggest stick she can build; she has no carrots to
dangle. Her dual economy means that North Korea has only two
diplomatic options: forward military deployment and the bomb.
She has no other leverage.

Because North Korea has her own considerable uranium mines,
she has the potential to develop more leverage there. She also has
significant stockpiles of chemical and biological weapons. She can
unleash bubonic plague, sarin nerve gas and a range of other lethal
cocktails. Her development of sophisticated missile delivery

systems—and Japan's weak responses—must be seen in that light. North Korea, a tin-pot, famine-ravaged nation run by unstable warmongers, regularly threatens Japan, the world's second largest economy with its primitive missiles. That threat has to be removed. TMD must be an integral part of that removal process.

Japan, as we have already seen, needs a regional missile defense system. Although missiles have been around since World War II, no one has yet developed a working defense against them—an exception to the rule of war that defensive weapons soon evolve to neutralize offensive ones. The lone strategy that offers hope is Theater Missile Defense (TMD), America's plan for welding South Korea, Japan, and Taiwan into a regional defensive arrangement. Under TMD, the defending country would use satellite sensors to locate incoming missiles and then fire its own defensive missiles or laser weapons to shoot down the enemy's offensive ones. Because TMD does not come on the cheap, it rules out other defense options. Because of the exorbitant costs involved, Japan must give serious consideration to joining the U.S.-sponsored TMD system along with South Korea and Taiwan. Even though Taiwan is developing her own system independently from the rest, none of these would-be allies can do it autonomously; the cost is simply too great. Whatever about Taiwan, Japan would be better employed sinking her money into TMD than in bailing out North Korea with the massive contributions already demanded from her—over $1 billion alone just to close down North Korea's nuclear reactors.

TMD affords Japan the chance of forging strong regional alliance. This benefit comes with the considerable cost of alienating China. It also runs the risk of pushing North Korea over the brink. If North Korea goes over the brink, they would attack Japan.

North Korea's forward deployment strategy is equally risky. Her decades-old policy of keeping the entire peninsula in a state of high alert runs the risk of causing another outbreak of war. In this at least, North Korea has been consistent. Her total war policy has not changed much since 1975 when North Korean President

Kim Il-sung, on a visit to his Beijing paymasters, threatened total war on the peninsula. In his most famous ever sound bite, he promised to turn Seoul into a sea of fire when the circumstances warranted it.

Although Maoism has since waned in Beijing, Kim's threats still resonate throughout Northeast Asia—and further afield. They made the United States Secretary of State Henry Kissinger repeatedly reaffirm his country's commitment to defend South Korea at any cost. Departing from the long-standing U.S. policy of refusing to confirm or deny the location of their nuclear arsenal, the United States Secretary of Defense James R. Schlesinger publicly acknowledged that American nuclear weapons were based in South Korea and that the United States would be willing to use them if the North provoked a doomsday scenario.

This was pretty strong stuff from America and was an indication of just how strongly the United States feels on the issue. Just as in the Cuban missile crisis, North Korea and her paymasters could have called America's bluff. But America was not bluffing. Japan could therefore have found herself enmeshed in a nuclear war on her doorstep without the wherewithal to defend herself. That is an unenviable position. But it is also a situation Japan must begin to deal with.

Tokyo is not an unconcerned bystander, who can remain oblivious and impervious to whatever happens next door. Korea has the capacity to embroil Japan in any future conflict; North Korea, in an effort to whip up Korean nationalism, would see to that. To this end, North Korea's missiles would almost certainly target Japan's major cities. Failure to respond would send a clear signal that Japan would, in the final analysis, only use its checkbook to defend itself. China would take note of this and, in its own time, could conceivably put its own unsustainable demands on that checkbook. The Korean peninsula is so vital to Japan that it cannot afford any miscalculation to occur there. However, the loose cannon of North Korea makes rational calculations redundant.

North Korea is not an ordinary state by any stretch of the imagination. Because of this, it is not amenable to more normal or reasonable solutions. The soft landing enjoyed in Poland, Hungary and other parts of Eastern Europe is not for it. A harsher, bumpier and more dangerous landing is, given the caliber of Pyongyang's leadership, a far more likely scenario. North Korea is, in essence, a kleptocracy being run in the interests of the ruling family and their military henchmen. Famine is rampant, international food aid is diverted to the military that prefer to develop weapons of mass destruction than to feed their people. Talks with them are a question of talking softly to ward off their paranoia and carrying a very big stick to match their own very formidable ones. The trouble is that behind North Korea lurks even bigger sticks. China and Russia are still engaged in courting Pyongyang and their power plays make the situation even less predictable. They are blocking the emergence of a pro-U.S. Korea for their own hegemonic reasons. The dagger must stay to Japan's heart.

Although uncoupling North Korea from its two major backers is a diplomatic matter, North Korea's surreal internal system makes it a particularly delicate one. North Korea's anachronistic political structures have brought their own strange ramifications to bear on the long-suffering people of North Korea. Pyongyang has developed a bizarre form of Marxism-Leninism to justify the feudalistic father-to-son succession of power to Kim Jong-il from Kim Il-sung. In the process, they have literally deified father and son—and mother as well! The North Korean leadership has concocted a variety of absurd quasi-miraculous legends to idolize Kim Jong-il. The end result of this bizarre mixture of Maoist and Messianic beliefs is that, to an extent unparalleled anywhere else in the world, the North Korean people have been brainwashed to believe that Kim Il-sung is the embodiment of their nation's mystical and omnipotent soul. Although it is easy to scoff at such silly beliefs, their Red Flag ideology makes these legends a very potent fighting tool.

The personality cult of Kim Il-sung and his eldest son and

successor, Kim Jong-il, is a direct threat to Japan. North Korea spends more than four times the percentage Japan spends on defense on boosting the ego of one family. They spend far more, of course, on their own defense procurements—second only to Serbia among the nations of the earth. And, just like Serbia, North Korea is hardly a model of brotherly tolerance and fraternal love. The only love that manifests itself in North Korea is the love of martyrdom that has been inculcated into its people through the Juche ideology.

Having been originally launched to allow Kim Il-sung survive the anti-Stalin backlash of the 1950s, the Juche Ideology has been modernized by the ruling hierarchy in Pyongyang as an ideological weapon to justify its harsh dictatorship. Externally, the Juche Ideology has been used as an ideological tool to trigger a Communist revolution in the South. The Juche Ideology preached that the South should not be a "running dog" of Yankee capitalism but should instead join in the unification of the peninsula with its fraternal and fratricidal brothers in the North.

North Korea's "Fuehrer doctrine" strengthened this ideology and the leaders' control. According to Juche beliefs, Kim Il-sung and Kim Jong-il are the Su-ryong (literally "leader" or Fuehrer) who have god-like powers. This Fuehrer philosophy demands absolute allegiance to Kim Jong-il's idiosyncratic commands by his million-plus military personnel and all the 22 million plus inmates of his weird fiefdom. Under the Fuehrer doctrine, the leader, Kim Il-sung and later, his son and heir, Kim Jong-il, are the queen bees, the reasons the others exist. The rest of the people only get their rationale for existence by how they relate to their Fuehrer and the political party surrounding him. It is a lethal brew.

The North Korean people have been indoctrinated to believe that national reunification can come only under the leadership of their living god and the political apparatus which surrounds him. The goal of national reunification under the living god and his sycophants cannot be negotiated away at international peace talks even in the face of endemic starvation and international diplomatic, military and economic isolation. North Korea's elite has been bought off to play along with this line and the ordinary citizens have been brow-beaten into believing that serving the Juche cause is, literally, a sacred duty demanding the ultimate sacrifice.

The Red Flag Ideology calls upon the North Korean masses to embrace the Juche spirit of self-reliance and to literally become human bullets and human bombs to protect the Leader, the queen bee of their controlled lives. Politically, the Red Flag Ideology is simply a more radical version of Jucheism aimed at keeping North Korea's long-suffering citizens focused on ideas of revolutionary Juche purity and away from the wholesale misery their corrupt leaders have visited upon them. Tactically, it could prove very effective.

Oddly enough, however, for such an avowedly Marxist nationalist country, this spirit of turning people into human bombs is a direct legacy of the Japanese imperial occupation. Like today's North Koreans, the Japanese used "the spirit of human bombs" in the context of radical allegiance to and worship of Hirohito, a god-king of their own, during the Pacific War. Just as the North Koreans have enveloped this suicidal tactic within the revolutionary sheen of the red flag, so also did the Imperial Japanese Army enwrap theirs in the ancient samurai code of bushido, the chivalric warrior code which predominated in Japan centuries ago.

Imperial Japan initiated an entire military campaign, which blended deliberate suicide in battle and religious emperor-worship into a standard military tactic. In doing so, Japan's suicide tactics tapped into a very potent cultural well. Suicide had long been elevated in Japanese samurai mythology and history. These traditions included the *hara-kiri* or *seppuku*, ritual suicide in expiation of dishonor or defeat and were integral to Japanese military strategy since January 8, 1940, when Japanese General Hideki Tojo ordered that the *Sen Jin Kun*, the Imperial Army's battle ethics, be distributed to all officers and men both at home and abroad. This order made the unwritten code of the samurai as interpreted by the Japanese High Command the required conduct of all Japanese servicemen. It ordered Japanese troops to embrace death warmly for the sake of the Emperor-god and of the nation. These battle rules and the indoctrination, which accompanied them, steeled the Japanese forces and made them difficult and infamously uncompromising enemies. The tactic proved especially useful in the dying days of the war. When the going got tough, the tough—and the suicide bombers—got going.

As the Japanese were continually pushed back towards their home islands, the Japanese Imperial general headquarters responded with even more extreme orders that made the battles for Okinawa and Iwo Jima, among others, particularly bloody. They ordered all of Japan's armed forces to emphasize suicide tactics. These tactics included not only the much publicized attacks by kamikazes and Baka bombs, but also suicide weapons platforms such as midget submarines with underwater fins, explosive motorboats, human torpedoes, human mines, suicide frogmen, glider-bombs, and mini-submarines, which would attach themselves and their explosives by suction or magnetic methods to enemy ships. If we exclude the plans to arm Japanese schoolchildren with sharpened bamboo sticks, the suicide charges in Okinawa were merely the last and most pathetic of these suicide tactics.

Crazy and all as they seem in hindsight, Japan had plenty of volunteers for these programs. The indoctrination campaign and the social stigma of shaming one's family by refusing a suicide mission saw to that. Although the number of volunteers waned as the end of the war drew near, none of the volunteers ever wavered when it came to the crunch. The hijacked bushido code saw that they obeyed their orders and went, lemming-like, to their ultimately futile deaths. The lessons of the kamikazes and of the bushido code, which controlled them, have been eagerly studied in North Korea. Pyongyang has followed Imperial Japan's path by elevating to the level of the divine, the teachings of Juche, the

Red Flag ideology and the personal oath of allegiance to their living god, Kim Jong-il, which all North Korea's armed forces are forced to take. Imperial Japan is not only the closer geographically to it. It is also the closest spiritually and historically.

The fanatical Red Flag ideology owes a lot to the duration and style of Japan's occupation of Korea. The 1904–05 Russo-Japanese war was, in large part, fought in northern Korea. By 1910, the Japanese had forced the abdication of the Korean king and had annexed the entire peninsula as a Japanese territory. Any sign of resistance was ruthlessly crushed. Cultural indoctrination was used to reinforce Japan's harsh rule. Shinto idolatry was enforced and all other forms of worship, Christianity in particular, were ruthlessly persecuted. Korean cultural traditions were forcibly replaced by their Japanese equivalents. When the Korean Christian churches finally capitulated in 1938, the peninsula had bowed to the full force of Japanese cultural indoctrination. An entire generation of Koreans was forced to partake in Shinto baptism and bow before Shinto shrines. These Shinto shrines were small houses with a picture of the Japanese emperor and his sun goddess consort. Each Korean home had to have one on prominent display in much the same way as each North Korean home must now display a picture and other icons of their current living god.

Warped Shintoism was not Japan's only cultural export to North Korea. The kamikaze tactic and the spirit of human bombs were others. Just as Japan continues to idolize its kamikaze pilots from the Pacific War, so also has North Korea begun the policy of deifying its own human bombs. This process began in 1998 when Kil Yong-jo was immortalized for using his plane as a human bomb. It is now an integral part of North Korea's battle plans. Although these are desperate tactics, they are sufficient to launch a major backlash that could engulf much of East Asia.

North Korea's suicide tactics could include some combination of air, surface, submarine, frogmen and terrorist forces on U.S. warships as well as Japanese and South Korean installations. Such terrorist type attacks would have the advantages of having a high-value impact for resources used without having the diplomatic fallout the use of nuclear, chemical or biological weapons of mass destruction would entail. However, when the human bomb tactic is added to the vast arsenal North Korea possesses, the threat becomes all the more ominous. Even the briefest review of North Korea's arsenal will show why this is so. North Korea is the world's third-ranking manufacturer and stock-piler of chemical weapons, next in size only to those of the United States and Russia. North Korea has concentrated its efforts on producing the most lethal cocktails imaginable. These include mustard gas, phosgene gas, sarin, and VM and VX gases.

Under normal circumstances, North Korea can produce about 5,000 tons of these gases a year, but in a war situation it will be capable of cranking out up to 12,000 tons a year. North Korea, in other words, has considerable capacity to conduct sustained chemical warfare. Although North Korea has probably between only 1,000 to 5,000 tons of these chemical weapons stockpiled, this gives it the capacity of exterminating 40 million people in the South. This is an extremely big and lethal stick. Her more conventional artillery pieces reinforce this threat. These latter include multi-rocket launchers, which are capable of delivering these chemical weapons throughout South Korea.

Nor is Japan immune from this threat. The 1,000–1,300 km range Rodong-1 missiles have the capacity of delivering these weapons even to Japanese territory. Because Japan and her allies can never hope to neutralize this threat without eliminating the Pyongyang regime as well, this means that North Korea will always be in a position to wave its big stick at Japan. It will also be able to point its missiles at Osaka, Tokyo and Japan's other great cities.

Although North Korea's chemical stockpiles of 5,000 tons might appear slight, a mere two tons of chemical weapons is enough to devastate Seoul or, indeed, Tokyo, which is now well within its range. North Korea has the capacity to deliver these weapons in a variety of ways, which include Red Flag bombers and FROG rockets. The North's AN-2 planes are of particular concern in this regard. They can infiltrate undetected into the South's airspace at night and drop chemical bombs on the population down below. Although these planes are difficult to detect under normal circumstances, the Red Flag ideology would make such considerations redundant in any event. Therefore, Pyongyang's chemical and biological capabilities, when added to its missile batteries and its Red Flag ideology, makes North Korea a very real threat to the future peace and prosperity of both South Korea and Japan.

Nor does the threat end there. North Korea's nuclear program will remain a threat as long as the regime continues in existence. Pyongyang's nuclear program has allowed it to make savings on its conventional forces and to give it extra leverage at the negotiating table as well. When coupled with its limited objective of forced Korean unification and its tactic of Red Flag fanaticism, this increased leverage gives North Korea international diplomatic leverage. They must be negotiated with to avoid them selling their secrets to others even more irrational than themselves. In this regard, North Korea's military links with the rogue nations of the Middle East become particularly problematic. The prospects of North Korea conducting secret sales of weapons in exchange for oil to those countries should also give Tokyo's security chiefs food for thought. More specifically, there are just too many wild cards outside of Tokyo's control floating about. The region is just too volatile.

And then there is Pyongyang's nuclear option. Because of its secret and duplicitous nature, it is difficult to accurately process North Korea's nuclear capability. Pyongyang only opened up its nuclear facilities for outside inspection on May 14, 1992. North Korea, tongue in cheek no doubt, stated that, though it was operating or constructing 16 separate nuclear facilities, it had no intention of building a bomb. It asked the world to take it at its word. Despite these massive expenditures, North Korea has constructed no nuclear power plant. Its protestations apart, the absence of a nuclear power plant can only mean one thing. North Korea has been operating these facilities for military purposes. That is, North Korea has been developing nuclear weapons of a rather crude nature. Although its devices are probably the crudest of all the nuclear powers, one important factor to bear in mind is that Pyongyang most likely lacks sufficient control systems similar to the very stringent black box digit code prepared for the exclusive use of the United States president. Because North Korea is a closed and irrational country, this is particularly threatening. They could, in other words, unleash their nuclear warheads by either accident or design. The cavalier fashion in which they lobbed test missiles over Japan only reinforces this scenario. North Korea's leaders simply cannot be trusted to act responsibly.

If all of the above were not bad enough, the North Koreans have other nasty packets as well as their nuclear and chemical ones. North Korea's biological weapons' program has concentrated on developing 11 particularly virulent kinds of germs: cholera, pest, anthrax, typhoid, yato, dysentery, diphtheria, typhus, tuberculosis, hepatitis, and brucellosis. North Korea's irrational leadership might decide to launch these against either South Korea or Japan simply to cause social confusion. Once again, North Korea has a high capability, this time in germ warfare technology, that Japan and other countries would be ill advised to ignore. Pyongyang could easily get enough Red Flag ideologues to do their gruesome job for them. Again, Japan would have to develop effective response measures. The evidence from the Aum sarin gas case, discussed in our penultimate chapter, is that Tokyo has still not got the stomach to resist.

Despite its formidable array of weapons of mass destruction, North Korea's missile technology is the most worrying aspect of them all. Pyongyang has a distinct advantage over the South in this regard. The North exported 100 SCUD-B missiles to Iran in 1987—evidence, at least, that Tehran values its expertise. These exports will continue to grow as North Korea's expertise grows. So too will the threats they pose to Japan and other countries in the more localized arena of the Korean peninsula.

When looked at in this light, North Korea's negotiating strategy becomes extraordinarily consistent and surprisingly successful. Although it brings little except its military muscle to the table, it succeeds in focusing the world's attention on its demands, and it consistently wins substantial concessions from Japan and the other Western allies. Pyongyang's negotiations are premised on the intertwining objectives of reinforcing domestic political control, securing pecuniary advantage, and disarming and confounding its enemies. Meanwhile, Japan and her allies have premised their negotiating policy on the rather naïve assumption that the Sunshine policy will cause North Korea's behavior to improve.

The West believes this because it wants to. The other, ultimately more rational, scenario just does not bring any soft options with it. North Korea is able to use the negotiations to fortify domestic control and to secure pecuniary advantage—including over $210 million in aid that the United States administration now extends to the regime annually. As if the idea of the United States handing over such a wad of money to the world's most repressive regime was not bizarre enough, the United States, Japan and their allies have also offered North Korea nuclear reactors worth over $5 billion in exchange for worthless North Korean commitments to promote North-South dialogue, advance international non-proliferation objectives, and freeze its graphite-moderated nuclear generating plants. The West will, in other words, give North Korea something tangible—$5 billion worth of nuclear reactors. In return, North Korea is asked to talk and to suspend its nuclear program.

Contrary to expectations, however, appeasement has not mollified North Korea. Pyongyang has used the years following the agreed framework on nuclear disarmament to develop the much more threatening military punch we have already outlined. She keeps the West guessing about her nuclear, biological and chemical intentions and, in the meantime, she builds up her conventional forces along with her missiles.

Japan is very uneasy with North Korea's missile tests and has repeatedly warned Pyongyang that it will suspend aid to North Korea if it continues its ballistic missile tests. This would include suspension of Japan's $1 billion contribution to the international consortium building two nuclear reactors for North Korea if it freezes its nuclear program. Pyongyang's launch of a rocket over Japan into the Pacific Ocean shocked Tokyo out of its benevolent complacency and worsened the already fragile relations between the countries. Tokyo's threat of withdrawing its financial aid notwithstanding, this provocative act had several advantages from North Korea's viewpoint. As well as securing increased orders for its missiles from the Middle East, it gave North Korea a new bargaining tool. Now the West must negotiate missiles as well as nuclear and other weapons with Pyongyang.

True to form and contrary to the evidence, Pyongyang insists it fired a satellite, not a missile. Whatever they fired, Japan's defense planners finally woke up. Tokyo put four satellites into orbit after North Korea test-fired the rocket over Japanese territory. The Japanese government found itself in the embarrassing position of relying on United States intelligence after failing to detect the launch, which was, of course, a direct threat to Japan's national security. North Korea, again true to form, is now using Japan's "aggression" as a bargaining chip and extracting more monetary concessions as a result.

North Korea's tests also spurred the South Korean and Japanese defense forces to hold limited joint exercises in August 1999. Given their historical enmity towards each other, this was a monumental policy change. The notion of Japanese military personnel setting foot again on Korean soil was so alien that, even at the height of the Cold War, any such incursions were ceremonial, occasional, and unpublicized. Now that the two countries see the common threat North Korea poses, they are starting to cooperate to counter it. The 1999 exercises will, hopefully, lead to a joint involvement in TMD over time. Only TMD can keep the North

Korean regime firmly caged in.

The process of negotiation is, in other words, cleverly managed by North Korea to postpone war while it reinforces its military capability and pressures the West to disarm. The danger for the West is that war may in fact be inevitable, but it will come only at a time of North Korea's choosing, when North Korea has perfected its weaponry and can be confident of surviving, at whatever cost, the conflict. Its leaders can hardly be said to hold the consequences to its people in any regard. Survival for them would be sufficient.

North Korea regards Japan as a toothless tiger, a soft touch and nothing more. North Korea has gone to the very brink of war with the United States, which packs a much bigger punch than Tokyo ever will. As recently as 1994, the United States was on the verge of invading North Korea. President Bill Clinton approved the dispatch of substantial reinforcements to Korea, and America drew up contingency plans to attack the North's nuclear weapons complex. Nuclear war with North Korea was avoided only by the extraordinary private diplomatic initiative of former President Jimmy Carter. This initiative led to the current curious spectacle of the world's strongest democracies cajoling the unwilling and unstable tyrants of Pyongyang to negotiate an accommodation extending their regime's survival or, at least, cushioning its collapse. The United States and Japan seek an accommodation in order to avoid the violence they fear might accompany North Korea's decline. North Korea, in contrast, seeks to deny accommodation, and uses both collapse and the threat of war as leverage. They therefore get monetary and logistical aid from the West while continuing to maintain the world's most oppressive regime.

Whereas North Korea's national goal remains the forced annexation of the South through revolutionary means, the government in Seoul has declared that it will pursue reconciliatory policies toward the North. Under these Sunshine policies, Seoul has been providing the North with necessary material and food aid despite Pyongyang's consistently belligerent attitude. But the North is taking advantage of these conditions to strengthen its United Front tactics. Even as North Korea's famine continues, it has escalated anti-Seoul propaganda and continues to finance subversion in the South. Pyongyang continues to pour scarce finances into biting the hand that feeds it.

Because the Pyongyang authorities ensure that Korea remains a dagger at Japan's heart, Tokyo will need to revamp her military and diplomatic efforts to ward off any threat emanating from the Korean peninsula. Although Korea is an immediate source of worry, it is not the only one. The next chapter, which deals primarily with Taiwan, paints an equally troubling vista.

TAIWAN:
China's Rebel Province

China's determination to reincorporate Taiwan into its regime makes a major regional war involving Japan almost inevitable. China labels Taiwan a renegade province and has repeatedly stated its determination to conquer it when the time is right. Former Chinese dictator Deng Xiaoping spelled out the five scenarios under which China would invade Taiwan. They are the development of a Taiwanese nuclear deterrent; a Taiwan-Russia entente; widescale Taiwanese unrest; a declaration of Taiwanese independence; or a rejection by Taipei of unification talks for a long time. In other words, if China feels that conquest by consent is not on the cards, or that Taiwan's power to resist will outpace their power to conquer, Beijing will invade, even if that means fighting formidable adversaries such as Russia. Or indeed Japan!

Whatever about closer ties with Japan, the prospects of a Taiwanese-Russian entente are very remote. China's diplomatic pressure has all but isolated Taiwan on the international diplomatic stage. Taiwan has been expelled from the United Nations to mollify

Beijing and China's veto guarantees that readmission is a non-starter. Less than 30 countries currently recognize Taiwan and, the Pope's mercurial battalions aside, none of those countries wields much power beyond their own largely irrelevant borders. These countries include Grenada, Belize, Haiti, the Dominican Republic, Honduras, Paraguay, Nicaragua, Chad, Malawi, The Vatican, Niger, Nauru, Tuvalu, Saint Christopher and Nevis, Liberia, and most recently, Macedonia. These countries are known more for their exotic postage stamps than for the power and influence they command in international affairs. They are bought off by Taiwan which, pathetically enough, welcomes East Timorese independence as it hopes the minnow former Portuguese colony will recognize it. Several other countries—Papua New Guinea, Guatemala, and the Bahamas among them—waver between recognition and non-recognition. Other countries, Australia, most notably, warn supposedly sovereign nations like Papua New Guinea not to recognize Taiwan for fear of economic retaliation from Beijing. Thus, as Australia's moral cowardice so amply illustrates, although Taiwan's vast foreign exchange reserves will allow her to retain some small pools of diplomatic recognition in the world's backwaters, the commercial and military might of the People's Republic of China will stop this recognition gaining critical mass in the international arenas that count.

Most countries will not recognize Taiwan for fear of angering China—and getting lectures from Australia. When China severs the political, economic and military ties that bind Taiwan to the region's major powers, the United States and Japan in particular, it will absorb Taiwan into Greater China—whether the Taiwanese want to join them or not. Whatever about Taiwan's legion of tiny states, this would have major repercussions for Taiwan's previous imperial master, Japan. It would show how weak Japan is even in her own backyard. It would mean that China's star would be in the ascendant in the region. Japan, by contrast, would be marginalized.

The odd thing about all of this is that China's claims to Taiwan are nebulous enough in the first place. They are roughly akin to her claims over Tibet, where she continues her harsh oppression unimpeded and undeterred by any outside force. China only first claimed Taiwan in 1887, when the Manchu Emperor—in a futile attempt to stop the Japanese expansion toward the south—suddenly, and to the surprise of all, declared the island to be a province of China. The Japanese ignored them and colonized the island—and later much of mainland China as well.

Chinese claims to the island therefore go back at most a little over a hundred years. They have negligible historical validity beyond that. When the Dutch East India Company landed on Taiwan in 1624, they encountered very few Chinese living on the island, and there was no Chinese administrative structure to speak of at all. China, unlike Japan, never properly occupied the islands. Like the islands of the South China Sea, Taiwan is only a recent addition to Beijing's Greater China shopping list.

Once Taiwan joins the Chinese fold, the Spratlys and other juicy tit-bits will quickly follow. China's territorial conquests will create their own imperative and, in the process, relegate Japan to a minor regional role. Japan's diplomatic lethargy will force her to have to live with the consequences of Chinese regional hegemony in the future. The failures of yesteryear will come back to haunt Tokyo.

This is all the legacy of Asia's sad history. In bleeding China dry, the European and American imperial powers left a vacuum in Asia, which Japan notoriously tried to fill during the 1930s and 1940s. The settlement that followed Japan's surrender created an artificial framework, which put the United States at the center of Asia and, perversely enough in retrospect, marginalized China, Asia's Middle Kingdom. Today's tensions are as much an effort to clean up these mistakes and oversights of history as they are to impose a new hegemony on the area. China does not want to be pushed about any more. She will certainly not be pushed about over Taiwan which, she feels, she has been wrongly denied by America and her allies.

When Japan abandoned Taiwan in 1945, they dealt exclusively with McArthur's American forces; they certainly never discussed Taiwan with the feuding Chinese parties on the mainland. The Chinese Nationalist forces only occupied Taiwan because McArthur personally ordered Chiang Kai-shek's forces to occupy the island on behalf of the Allied forces: he did not cede the island to them but merely asked his Chinese allies to take some of the manpower pressures off his own troops, who had the potentially much more dangerous prospect of occupying Japan to keep them on their toes. As far as McArthur was concerned, the issue of Taiwanese sovereignty had still to be settled. He did not cede it to China. Nor did anyone else.

Japan only ceded sovereignty over Taiwan at the 1951 San Francisco Peace Conference. This comprehensive treaty did not name any beneficiary. The treaty instead left Taiwan's fate to a future decision by the people of Taiwan in accordance with the purposes and principles of the Charter of the United Nations. Under this charter, the Taiwanese should have been allowed to decide their own fate. Instead Taiwan faced prolonged threats of imminent invasion from Beijing. Having been subjected to the violence of Chiang Kai-shek's forces, the Taiwanese have shown no great fervor to have the People's Liberation Army visit them as well. They have instead opted for independence. In an ideal world, the PRC should respect that decision. They should not go where they are not wanted.

This, unfortunately, is not an ideal world, partly because of the considerable power the PRC wields. When Beijing maneuvered the Carter administration to recognize them as the legitimate masters of China and to sever their diplomatic relations with Taipei, the United States Congress passed the Taiwan Relations Act to reaffirm the close cultural and economic ties between the United States and Taiwan. Most importantly for our purposes, the Taiwan

Relations Act stated that the United States would continue to arm Taiwan, and that Taiwan's political future could only be decided by peaceful means. Implicit in this was the American threat to go to war to defend Taiwan. America, in other words, has implied that it is prepared to go to war with the nuclear power of China over Taiwan. As part of this commitment, the United States Seventh Fleet has faced down the Chinese Navy on several occasions in the Taiwan Strait.

China takes that entire argument with a hefty pinch of salt. The world now recognizes that there is one China, not two. That being so, Beijing, not Taipei, must be the capital. The issue then is not whether there is one China or two but how to reincorporate Taiwan into the bosom of the mainland. Although Beijing would like Taiwan to fall peacefully into her lap like Hong Kong and Macao did, if push ever comes to shove, Beijing has made it patently clear that it is prepared to shove back. This is a stylized fact, one Japan must remember when dealing with its giant neighbor over the coming years.

Because America's commitment will waver in the years to come, all of this is of direct concern to Japan, which will have to choose between the two Chinas. China is now the much larger trading partner for Japan, while Taiwan continues to struggle in an increasingly hostile world levered by an increasingly irritated Beijing into isolating Taipei. Although Beijing's leaders continue to harangue Taipei's thirty or so minnow diplomatic allies, they are much more concerned with Taiwan's unofficial links with Japan and the United States. Beijing knows that it is easier to lean on Tokyo, which is the weaker of the two. Certainly, Washington has proved its mettle much more so than Japan in the disputes, which have punctuated the Taiwan Straits standoff since the time of the San Francisco treaty. If Tokyo could be got to abandon Taipei, Washington would most likely follow. Either way, a weakening of the Japan-America alliance would only aid Beijing in its struggle against Taipei.

Therefore, as part of this process of selective pressure, Beijing tries to stop Japan's airlines, media companies and banks operating in Taipei by curtailing their rights in mainland China. China is prepared to lean on Japanese companies to force Tokyo to abandon Taipei. The longer-term quid pro quo is a license to operate in China for agreeing to China's Taiwan policy. All of that is in the future. For the moment, Beijing wants Japan to accept the "three nos" on Taiwan: no to the two Chinas policy, no to Taiwan's independence and no to Taiwan's involvement in international organizations made up of sovereign states. The implications these Japanese acts of appeasement entail are immense. Excluding Taiwan from international financial organizations, for example, is nonsensical. Taiwan has one of the world's largest caches of foreign exchange reserves and it is the strongest of all the Asian tiger economies. It is one of the world's largest and most important economies, whose sole sin is the enmity Beijing feels towards it. Isolating Taiwan diplomatically will eventually allow China's policy to succeed. Taiwan will be incorporated into China, the islands of the South China Sea will follow and there will be no buffer state left between Japan and China. This would prove ominous for Japan. Historically, it would be akin to the unification and subsequent rise of Germany in the nineteenth century. Just as Germany had to fight with all her neighbors, so also, in the absence of buffer states, would an expanded China be expected to clash with a marginalized Japan. Lacking the infrastructure of the EU, East Asia would only become more unstable than it already is. This would not be in Japan's interest.

Japan must formulate its Taiwanese policy and be prepared for the consequences. If Japan wants to be a regional force, she must bite the bullet on Taiwan. Although the situation in the Taiwan Strait remains tense, there is still time for Japan to formulate the correct response: to join Taiwan and the United States in the TMD program and to partake in relevant defense treaties as well. Taiwan can only be saved over the longer haul by Japan, South

Korea and other regional countries adopting a more forceful presence through TMD in their own backyard. Even at that, Taiwan's future and, by extension, Japan's, is not fully secure. The sheer size of the PLA sees to that.

If luck is on the side of the big battalions, the PLA must have all the luck in the world. Currently, China's more than 2.5-million-man PLA dwarfs Taiwan's defense force of about 400,000. In most cases, equipment totals are similarly lopsided in favor of the PLA. China has nearly 4,500 combat aircraft, as compared with some 400 on Taiwan. The Chinese Navy has about 65 attack submarines—five of which are nuclear powered—as compared with Taiwan's derisory four diesel powered submarines. China has over 60 major surface combatants while Taiwan has less than 40. China has nuclear weapons and a ballistic missile force that can deliver nuclear or conventionally armed warheads almost at will into any region of Taiwan.

The contest between China and Taiwan is like that between David and Goliath, with several important caveats thrown in. Whereas David relied on speed and on Goliath's over-confidence, China, Goliath's equivalent in this dispute, is much more cautious. Similarly, whereas David felled Goliath with one well-aimed slingshot to the head, Taiwan, David's equivalent in this fight, does not possess a single magic bullet. Unlike the biblical clash, the struggle between Taiwan and the PRC will most likely be a long one where a variety of weapons and strategies will be employed. Further, unlike the biblical tale, Taiwan, David's equivalent, is unlikely to win with a lucky shot. Taiwan can only play for time and hope against apparent hope that China will somehow reform in the interim.

Therefore, although the numbers are overwhelmingly on Beijing's side, China currently does not have the capability to invade and conquer Taiwan. The Chinese armed forces could not currently implement what would be one of the largest amphibious assaults in history—comparable in size to the D-Day Normandy landings but infinitely more difficult in execution. Unlike the D-Day assault on Normandy, Taiwan is simply too far away from the Chinese mainland—the Chinese would have to cross at least 80 to 100 miles of open sea to reach their heavily fortified target. Even assuming that they could win air superiority over the Taiwan Strait, the Chinese do not have the amphibious vessels to ferry the more than 250,000 troops that a successful invasion would require across this stretch of water. Logistically, the problem is currently too intractable for the Chinese. They would need several hundred landing vessels to ferry their assault forces across the Strait—currently they have only 70 such vessels. Nor could they mass sufficient sophisticated aircraft to attain the necessary air superiority over the Taiwan Strait during the invasion.

Achieving and then maintaining air superiority over the Taiwan Strait would be a crucial component of any proposed Chinese military invasion of Taiwan. Although China's air force currently vastly outnumbers Taiwan's, Taiwan's packs the more solid punch. However, because the PLA would employ widescale sabotage operations and missile strikes, the air advantage would lie with China in any drawn-out confrontation that did not suck in the United States and regional powers such as Japan.

Once the PLA neutralized Taiwan's air defenses, they would be well on the way to over-running the island. Having executed a blockade of the island, China's air forces would achieve air superiority by a war of attrition. Naval assaults, missile attacks and port mining by China's formidable submarine fleet would eventually whittle away Taiwan's navy. Airborne, airmobile and special operations forces would conduct simultaneous attacks to the rear of Taiwan's coastal defenses to seize a port, preferably in close proximity to an airfield. Other PLA units would seize beachheads in supporting attacks. An airborne envelopment would facilitate amphibious operations by cutting off Taiwan's coastal defenders from supply lines and forcing them to fight in two directions. The pressure would be relentless.

Beijing's suppression of Taiwan's air defenses would be quickly followed by a second-wave air attack, which would establish air superiority over an invasion corridor in the Taiwan Strait. Priority for air defense protection and fighter escort operations would shift from bombers carrying anti-ship cruise missile (ASCM) to fixed—and rotary-wing transports ferrying additional airborne and airmobile assault forces. Both China's military and merchant vessels would join the invading armada. China would also saturate the Taiwan Strait with numerous civilian merchant and fishing vessels; this would confuse and eventually overwhelm Taipei's surveillance and target acquisition systems. The PRC would then go on to consolidate and expand their toehold on the rebel province.

The PLA's success in establishing and maintaining a foothold on Taiwan would rest on a wide variety of intangibles. These would include morale, attrition rates and the ability of both sides to maintain operations. Once Chinese forces landed, one thing would be definite. It would be a bloody fight to the finish with no quarter and, therefore, no outside intervention. Taiwan would stand but most likely die alone. Given Beijing's overwhelming numerical superiority, the odds are that once the beachhead was established, the PLA would prevail.

In order for an invasion to ultimately succeed, Beijing would have to conduct a multi-faceted campaign including air assaults, airborne insertions of Taiwanese space, special operations raids behind Taiwanese lines, amphibious landings, maritime area denial operations, air superiority operations and conventional missile strikes. Although the PLA would encounter great difficulty in conducting such a sophisticated campaign over the next decade, she will improve her capability with time. Time is, after all, on her side. So too are the numbers—and the world's diplomatic community. Eventually, only Japan and the United States could stop the takeover. Taiwan could not hope to stand alone.

Taiwan's air force has over 500 combat aircraft and these include top of the range U.S. F-16s and French Mirage 2000-5s.

Taiwan's air defenses are so strong that China could not hope to launch an effective air campaign in the near future. Taiwan's 68,000-strong navy has more than 36 frigates and destroyers as well as four submarines and would wreak havoc on a Chinese invasion armada under current conditions. Behind Taipei's well-honed stick stands the awesome armada of the Japanese-based U.S. Seventh Fleet together with its carrier battle groups, which can be quickly deployed into Taiwanese waters. China is currently powerless against the Seventh Fleet. Therefore, as long as America continues to underwrite Taiwan's security, a direct invasion is not a credible possibility. However, the continued presence of the U.S. Seventh Fleet as a protective umbrella cannot be taken for granted. When the Seventh Fleet goes, so too will Taiwan, Asia's key buffer state.

Taiwan is the domino state. If Taiwan falls, the islands of the South China Sea will be in China's direct line of fire. Over time, China would be expected to increase the heat there, too, and thereby put the navies of China and Japan on a collision course with each other. Japan therefore cannot ignore Taiwan's fate. Taiwan's independence is a vital issue for Japan, one for which she must be prepared to fight to preserve. The fate of Taiwan is of vital national interest to Japan. Rhetoric apart, Japan cannot afford to allow China to swallow up the island.

However, Japan is currently powerless to stop China. All Tokyo can do is join TMD and begin to develop a diplomatic strategy. Tokyo must become more engaged with China. She must understand China's position: that Taiwan is an integral part of China and that, subject to logistical constraints and the five caveats already described, China is prepared to go to war to resolve the issue. And then Japan must get the two Chinas to the negotiating table.

This is because Japan must watch the dynamics of Taiwan's fate very closely. Having been caught unawares by Pyongyang's missiles, she cannot afford to be outflanked by Taiwan's fate. Just like Germany in the closing days of the nineteenth century, China sees itself engaged in nation building on a massive scale. And just like Germany, there are countervailing forces at work. There are two forces that can check China. These are a resurgent Japan and the security umbrella the U.S. Seventh Fleet bestows. China's tactics are designed to either unhinge or puncture that umbrella over time; its diplomatic tactics are likewise designed to weaken the shield by pressurizing America to sail home to Hawaii. Just like Germany's tactics, China's are designed to guarantee her sovereignty. Just like Germany, they also involve China clashing with her many neighbors. All of these factors must be considered when we observe Beijing's war games in the Taiwan Strait.

Although Beijing might impose a sustained sea and air blockade to destroy Taiwan's economy, China just does not presently have the logistical capabilities for such an extended campaign. China's best tactic for the moment is the hit and run tactics she is currently employing. Like North Korea, she can create anxiety and then let the anxiety subside until it suits her interests to escalate it once more. Beijing's calculated build-up is geared to foster anxiety in Taiwan and consternation among her allies. China's large submarine force, augmented with Russian Kilo-class vessels, is designed to bring Taiwan to the negotiating table. Beijing is not so much aiming for immediate military conquest as it is to softening up Taiwan and her allies by causing economic panic and economic chaos on the island. Though Beijing's recent military exercises in the Taiwan Straits were amateurish in part and showed that China just does not have the capability at present to invade Taiwan, they had the desired social impact. The Taipei stock market went into a tailspin every time new tests were announced. Rice buying panics caused social unease and unrest.

China was well pleased with the results, which ensure the question of unification stays on the front burner. In the future, China can adopt a mixture of missile tests, sea blockades, combined force drills and military build-ups to rattle the "renegade province." For example, a maritime blockade of Taiwan's major two ports of

Keelung in the north and Kaohsiung in the south would cause insurance rates to skyrocket. As well as diverting trade to the mainland, this would have the advantage of eroding and eventually undermining Taipei's credibility. Even if such a blockade only lasted for a couple of weeks, the net effect of all of this would be to further destabilize Taipei and discourage major foreign support and investment from countries such as Japan.

The primary intent behind such a blockade of the island would be to cripple Taiwan economically and further isolate it internationally. Beijing would choose successively more stringent quarantine-blockade actions, beginning with declaring maritime exercise closure areas and impounding Taiwan-flagged merchant vessels operating in the Taiwan Strait. Chinese coastguards have already begun this softening up process. In late July 1999, they grabbed a Taiwanese ship, which was transporting food supplies to soldiers on Taiwan's front-line islands, and forced it to go to the mainland instead. China will continue these tactics to soften up Taipei and force countries like Japan to give the beleaguered island a wide berth. These tactics keep Taiwan unsettled. Taipei is powerless to respond: it can hardly threaten to invade the mainland in retaliation. The balance of fear, in other words, overwhelmingly lies with Beijing, which has the option to increase the psychological pressure on Taipei any time it chooses.

China's increase of troops and missiles in the so-called Nanjing War Zone across from Taiwan are another major psychological card in China's hand. This buildup is designed to cause further long-term anxiety and unease in Taiwan. The Chinese military has stationed 150 to 200 M-9 and M-11 missiles in its southern regions aimed at Taiwan. The M-9 is capable of delivering a 500-kilogram payload over a range of 600 kilometers. The M-11 has a shorter range but can deliver a larger payload. Both are capable of carrying nuclear warheads. All of this must give cause for concern in Taipei—and in Tokyo and any other center that might find itself on Beijing's hit list in the future.

China's missile threat to the entire region will only escalate until TMD, combined with diplomatic efforts, unite to neutralize it. China views its growing conventionally armed ballistic missile force as a potent military and political weapon to cow Taiwan's populace and their leaders. China is expending vast sums developing and perfecting her wide array of missiles. Soon, all of Taiwan will be within range of these weapons of mass destruction unless TMD becomes operational.

Japan, which has its own territorial disputes with Beijing, can have no doubt about China's intentions. Within the next decade, China's missile forces will be sufficiently large to target all of Taipei's air defense installations, airfields, naval bases and other vital facilities. China is also conducting an aggressive effort to acquire foreign cruise missile technology and subsystems, particularly from Russia and Israel. China's ASCM capability will improve further with the planned acquisition of two Russian-built Sovremenny-class destroyers armed with state of the art ASCM systems.

China, in short, is devoting vast resources to her missile program. This is a war of nerves where time and, ultimately, technology, is on the side of Mainland China's leaders. This psychological aspect explains China's widespread use of ballistic missiles, which are, in essence, really psychological weapons—paper tigers if you will. Although Taiwan can protect itself from an amphibious assault, protecting Taipei from surgical missile strikes—or the threat of surgical strikes—by Beijing's ballistic missile units is a more daunting task. Beijing knows this and will continue to tighten and loosen the screws, as she deems appropriate.

This fits into China's policy of achieving its regional objectives on the cheap. The balance of fear lies with China and against America and her regional allies, Japan included. America is tied to Asia by policy only: the Seventh Fleet can always withdraw to Hawaii. Not so Japan, Taiwan, and South Korea. Because they are integral parts of Asia, they will have to live with the consequences of an American withdrawal and consequent Chinese hegemony.

If America can be ushered out of Asia and if TMD is not implemented, China's missile campaign will give Beijing hegemony by default.

Japan must take all of this into account. She must join TMD to achieve a parity of fear. Because China cannot be militarily defeated, Japan must work to achieve a peaceful resolution of the issue. She must also begin to talk with China to avoid strategic miscalculations. Japan must work to establish frameworks along the lines of the EU and NATO to allow these differing world-views to be accommodated. Otherwise, war will result.

The implications are particularly ominous for Taiwan, which depends on its modern infrastructure to maintain its place in the world. With a mere forty-five missiles, China could obliterate Taiwan's ports, airfields, waterworks, and power plants, and destroy the oil-storage facilities of the island nation, which depends on continual replenishment of its oil supplies from the outside world to thrive. Accurate missiles would destroy this infrastructure with minimal civilian casualties, using conventional warheads in attacks no larger than those the United States launched against Iraq on several occasions since the Gulf War ended. China can, under this scenario, engineer a situation where the international community's silence will implicitly condone such attacks on her isolated "renegade" province.

This would undermine Taiwan's entire defense plans. Although Taiwan has purchased a handful of Patriot Pak 11 missile batteries from the United States, it needs scores more to defend the entire island. Because Taiwan lacks the satellite-communication links to give early warning in case of an attack, her missile defenses are very limited. Taiwan is, in other words, at the mercy of China's ballistic missile blackmail.

So too is the United States, which has a legal obligation to Taiwan under the Taiwan Relations Act of 1979. China is busy pushing the United States into abandoning its commitment to Taiwan. Because time is on her side, China uses the carrot and the stick.

The PLA wave China's array of sticks and the sheer size of China's markets represent the juicy carrot. America's Chamber of Commerce has concentrated more on the fat carrot than the bundle of sticks. Eager to win supposedly lucrative contracts for its members, the Chamber retains Henry Kissinger and other famous diplomats to carry China's cause into America's most exalted corridors of power. These apostles of engagement downplay China's growing military might as well as her abysmal human rights record and, in the process, they make Taiwan's cause more precarious than it already is. China, needless to say, is pleased with the results.

When taken together with its gunboat diplomacy in the Spratlys and the Korean standoff, the stakes are much bigger than the fate of one renegade province. China's ultimate prize is East Asian hegemony, which is probably inevitable in any event. China's eventual regional ascendancy will spell the end of the Pax Americana in East Asia. Japan will thus find itself in the position of being beholden to a large and potentially hostile power with America's Seventh Fleet scurrying back home to Hawaii. This will totally transform the socio-political status quo in the region. From the end of World War II, the United States has militarily dominated Asia by operating from forward bases that were secure from attack and by sailing convoys of warships that were immune from any form of attack. With the increased reach of Chinese missiles, this era is now rapidly coming to a close. Again, although this might be no bad thing, Japan is singularly unprepared for the diplomatic complexities China's inevitable ascendancy gives rise to. Not only is the imperative with China but Japan stands confused and, most likely, eventually alone.

China's capacity to strike, as distinct from actually striking, will force the United States forces and Japan and the other nations that host them to think twice about reinforcing forward bases in the first place, if doing so might trigger a Chinese attack and a major escalation of tensions in the region. Forward deployments or even reinforcing Okinawa and other sounding stations will thus increasingly be seen as likelier to escalate a crisis than to dampen it. Reluctance to run the risk of drawing Chinese fire will strain the most breakable part of forward engagement—host-nation political approval.

The main host nation in the region is Japan. Chinese pressure, when combined with the misguided antics of Japan's political hawks, could swing the pendulum irrevocably against having American bases in Japan. Though such a scenario might have appeal to Japanese hawks, it would have even greater attractions to their Chinese counterparts. The end of American bases in Japan would put China's hawks, not Japan's hawks, in the ascendant. Although Japan's hawks might sing, they would not be able to fly. The skies and everything beneath them would belong to China.

Japan, as later chapters will show, is in no position to engage in an arms race with China. Although Japan must beef up her military muscles, these must be used to complement a diplomatic initiative, which has to be Tokyo's trump card. Japan, as well as being prepared for war-war, must hone up her skills of jaw-jaw. The Taiwan debacle could well entail her employing both of these long somnolent skills. Certainly, if Japan does not become more diplomatically involved with China, she will have to be prepared for war.

China will no doubt raise the stakes over Taiwan in the future. Beijing's missiles will add new dimensions to her successful tactics of isolating Taiwan that she has relentlessly employed over the last 40 years. If Tokyo blinks in the face of these missiles and closes Okinawa and other bases, the future of East Asia will be in China's hands. Japan will stand isolated, emasculated and alone. The fall of Taiwan would, in other words, mean the fall of the United States in the entire region. Such an outcome would have to be blamed on Taiwan's two major unofficial allies—Japan and the United States. Expediency and hand-ringing apart, the fault could not be laid at Taipei's door. Taiwan is already doing all she can do to defend herself against the world's largest army. Current

Taiwanese missile defenses center on the U.S. Patriot Pac 11 and Taiwan's own Tien Kung 11. Both give about 2 minutes—120 seconds—prior warning of the doom to follow. Only TMD can extend that time window to something more realistic.

That is assuming that China does not upgrade her military capacity. China is being supplied with arms and technological transfers from Israel, Russia, France, Germany, and Britain, among others. Russia has supplied two Sovremenny class destroyers as well as the technology for ship to ship and air to air missiles. Taiwan is matching this threat with considerable expenditures from France and Germany as well as an escalated ship-building program of its own. All of this means that the conflict, if it comes, will employ the world's best and most sophisticated weaponry on both sides. This being so, the risks of a hot war are all the higher.

Although Taipei's air force has some 150 U.S.-made F-16s, 60 French Mirage 2000-5s jets, and 130 locally developed Indigenous Defense Fighters, the military balance between the PRC and Taiwan is shifting toward Beijing. Beijing has protested long and hard about America's sale of F-16s to Taiwan and has bought her way into the U.S. Democratic Party to ensure that there are no repeat sales—even as her spies buy and steal America's nuclear secrets. Eventually Beijing will cut off American military supplies to Taiwan altogether. Once isolated, Taipei will quickly capitulate.

Because Taiwan is determined to resist, she is pinning much of her hopes on TMD and the alliances with South Korea and Japan that are necessary to cement TMD. Japan, therefore, has the choice of maintaining Taiwan's current ambivalent status or surrendering her to Beijing. Whatever Tokyo decides, she must realize that there will be a price to pay. This is all the more so as China increasingly puts America on the back foot in Asia.

China has pushed Washington into an ever-diminishing diplomatic corner. As part of the One China policy dogma, the United States, having repeatedly committed itself to isolating Taiwan politically and diplomatically, is coming under mounting PRC pressure to help neuter the island's military capacity to defend itself. Paradoxically, the United States has repeatedly indicated that it would protect Taiwan with American firepower, even if it meant risking a war with Beijing. Eventually, the United States and Japan would be forced to choose between Taipei and Beijing. Failing a clear commitment to TMD, the two allies will have to eventually choose Beijing and all that that entails. Chinese pressure works slowly but constantly and confidently for this result.

Although America could abandon Taipei and face-save by increasing arms sales to it, this policy would only doom Taiwan to eventual rule by Beijing. Washington has sold Taipei an impressive array of weaponry over the last decade. These have included F-16 fighters, helicopters, and Stinger anti-aircraft missiles, Knox-class Navy frigates along with rapid-fire Phalanx anti-aircraft guns and Harpoon anti-ship missiles. However, the United States has thus far declined to approve sales of other crucial items, including the sophisticated AIM-120 Advanced Medium Range Air-to-Air Missile and advanced versions of the air-to-surface Maverick missile. The Taiwanese also want to buy attack submarines and develop, with United States assistance, an anti-ballistic-missile system, but Washington has thus far rebuffed both requests. Submarines are especially important to Taiwanese military planners because, unless Taipei upgrades its tiny submarine fleet, Beijing's navy will end up dominating the Taiwan Strait when the Seventh Fleet eventually withdraws its protection.

The PRC maintains an overwhelming and almost unassailable advantage in submarines over Taiwan and this quantitative advantage is unlikely to diminish in the years ahead. China is busily upgrading its submarine fleet and is buying state of the art submarine-related technology from Russia, which will help to expedite the process of forced unification. Although China's submarine force is oriented principally toward interdicting surface ships using torpedoes and mines, China now deploys submerge-launch YJ-62 cruise missiles on its submarine fleet. China's submarine fleet constitutes a formidable force capable of controlling sea lanes and mining approaches around Taiwan, as well as a growing threat to American and Japanese submarines in the East and South China Seas. China's submarine policy is, in other words, directly geared towards its regional territorial ambitions.

Taiwan, by contrast, has only four submarines: two relatively modern Dutch-built boats acquired in the late 1980s and two obsolete, World War II-era boats provided by the United States in 1973 of no great practical use. The two Dutch submarines are armed with wire-guided torpedoes. The U.S. boats are used primarily as training platforms with a secondary mission to lay mines. Acquisition of additional submarines remains one of Taiwan's most important priorities. The United States has so far refused to supply Taiwan with the submarines she needs to counter China's awesome armada. Japan could, of course, step into the breach here if she abandoned her embargo on exporting defense materiel. Because this latter move is unlikely over the shorter term, other scenarios must be considered.

One other option would be to draw Japan directly into the fray. Taiwan, along with Japan and South Korea, is included in the scope of a potential Theater Missile Defense (TMD) for the region. Because TMD would swing the balance of power decidedly away from Beijing, China has objected loudly to any such plans even reaching the planning stage: it would be years yet before they could be actually implemented. As part of its war of words, Chinese strategists are protesting that TMD is the latest step in a conspiracy to build a Pacific alliance against China, anchored by the United States, Japan, and South Korea, and now threatening to include Taiwan as well. There is much validity in this. Taipei, for example, would be delighted to pull South Korea and Japan, to say nothing of the United States, into its alliance: they would even up the numbers. In Taipei's view, TMD is not only a potential building block in its new goal of creating an impregnable Fortress Taiwan, but a way of recruiting new allies to its own defense and therefore of breaking out of the diplomatic straitjacket Beijing has put them in. TMD then, would change the balance of forces across the Taiwan Strait. Such a realignment would have regional and global ramifications that Japan could not ignore.

China's displays of military muscle-flexing have made TMD an urgent matter for Taipei. During their 1996 showdown, when China launched missile-firing exercises around Taiwan, the People's Liberation Army had deployed 30 to 40 DF-9 and DF-11 missiles along the coast facing Taipei. Now there are 120 to 150 mobile launchers. Given China's production capacity, that figure will most likely grow to 700 or more missiles over the next few years. China's military buildup is an awesome demonstration of military intention.

Although the United States and Japan continue to discuss the matter with China, they should be under no illusions. China cannot and will not abandon or downgrade its missile program. A short overview of Chinese strategy shows why. The PRC has historically maintained a large armed forces structure capable of responding to a wide range of perceived internal and external contingencies. These contingencies have ranged from the threats Vietnam, India and the former Soviet Union posed to dealing with Taiwan and the islands of the South China Sea. China has most recently been focusing primarily on preparing for military contingencies along its southeastern flank, especially in the Taiwan Strait and the South China Sea.

Although the PLA is still decades away from possessing a comprehensive capability to engage and defeat a modern adversary beyond China's boundaries, Beijing believes that Chairman Mao's military doctrine can be modified to meet modern conditions. The PLA has developed the theory of asymmetric advantage. The PLA can, in other words, develop asymmetric abilities in certain niches—such as advanced cruise missiles and conventional short-range ballistic missiles (SRBMs). Asymmetric warfare is a modern form of guerrilla warfare. It entails attacks by a weaker or more technologically backward opponent on a stronger foe's vulnerabilities using unexpected or innovative means, while avoiding the adversary's strengths. In this context, the objective would be to neutralize Taiwan's defenses with an unstoppable array of missiles and supporting hardware.

Within the next several years, the size of China's SRBM force will grow substantially. An expanded arsenal of conventional SRBMs and LACMs targeted against critical Taiwanese facilities will complicate Taipei's ability to conduct autonomous military operations. Although China would currently encounter problems coordinating missile firings with air and maritime engagements, these will be perfected over time. For Taipei, the prognosis, with or without TMD, is somewhat bleaker. Exclusive Taiwanese reliance on active missile defenses and associated materiel will not sufficiently offset the overwhelming advantage in offensive missiles, which Beijing will possess in the coming years. Unless TMD becomes an operational reality, Beijing will have to prevail in time. There is no other conclusion to be drawn.

Despite continued improvements to Taiwan's missile and air defense systems, the PLA will soon possess the capability to attack Taiwan with air and missile strikes which would degrade key military facilities and fatally damage the island's economic infrastructure. This makes China's preoccupation with long-range precision-strike programs very understandable. The PLA's obsession with missiles has wrecked Taipei's defense plans. These plans traditionally focused on three specific areas: maintaining air superiority over the Taiwan Strait and the waters contiguous to Taiwan; conducting effective counter-blockade operations; and defeating an amphibious and aerial assault on the island. Taipei hoped that its technological and tactical advantage over Beijing in these areas would buy it sufficient time until the forces of democracy won out in China.

To continue to buy time until Beijing democratizes, Taiwan's defenses will have to be able to protect the island primarily against missile attacks. Currently, this is impossible. Although successors to the U.S. Patriot missiles used against Iraqi Scuds in the Gulf War might neutralize the threat of short-range Chinese missiles traveling up to 300 kilometers, they wouldn't have the reach to defend Taiwan against medium-range Chinese missiles like the DF-21, which has a range of more than 2,000 kilometers. For those, Taiwan would need U.S. systems designed to intercept incoming missiles before they re-enter the Earth's atmosphere. The good news for Taiwan is that a single land base or ship could defend the entire island against anything Beijing could currently toss at it. The bad news is that the new U.S. land- and sea-based systems will not reach initial operational capability for at least another decade.

Taiwan must sweat out the intervening years and hope that Beijing does not manage to isolate her in the interim. Although Taiwan has pursued an aggressive policy of arms development herself, she still relies on the United States for key technology, especially in the field of advanced missile defenses. The importance of this is that Taiwan cannot develop an appropriate missile defense shield to China's growing missile threat without the support of outside partners to share the expenses and to develop the required expertise. Although the same, of course, is true of Japan, Taiwan's situation is more urgent. China's present missile buildup is designed to dissuade the United States from incorporating Taiwan under the defensive shield of the proposed East Asian Theater Missile Defense system.

Taiwan, Asia's key buffer state, will therefore have to remain on the defensive for the foreseeable future. Japan is in a slightly different position. It has many more variables to assess. Chief among these is the People's Republic of China. We next turn to an examination of that largest of all Asia's imponderables.

CHINA versus JAPAN

As the Cold War wanes, the shadow of China lengthens. China's population of 1.3 billion makes it the world's most populous country. China will be the world's largest economy in the next decade or two even if its current annual growth rates of over 10 percent eventually falter. China is already the second-largest economy in the world. China is a nuclear power. It holds a permanent seat on the United Nations Security Council. China is a regional power inexorably evolving into a world power.

China remains Asia's Middle Kingdom. It has vast land boundaries of some 17,000 miles with the fifteen countries it borders. It has territorial disputes with most of these as well as a range of maritime disputes with Malaysia, Brunei, the Philippines, Indonesia, Taiwan, Japan, and Vietnam among others. China has got its hands dirty in Tibet and Cambodia, and it has fought a major war in Korea. China's internal history over the last one hundred years has witnessed the biggest mass killings of all time. China is truly a power Japan has to reckon with.

Debate on China revolves around engagement versus containment. The containment lobby argues that China is an expansionist country that must be contained. The engagement lobby focuses on the crock of gold—China's vast markets—and argues that penetrating them will make political reform inevitable. These arguments have been heard before. In 1958, for example, China grew at 22 percent a year—at the height of Chairman Mao's Great Leap Forward. Those impressive growth rates were, like today, only one side of the Chinese coin. During the Great Leap Forward, China's Marxist policies sparked a man-made famine that killed 20 million Chinese civilians. The engagement arguments current now were current then as well. Despite the Maoist excesses, David Rockefeller and other leading American entrepreneurs were praising China's social engineering and arguing for engagement with Chairman Mao's evil empire. Despite today's headline grabbing growth, most Chinese people live in abject poverty. Today, China's per capita gross domestic product remains below those of Libya, Albania, Colombia, and Bostwana. Its human rights record remains similarly unimpressive. And the same debate about engagement or containment rages.

China is unquestionably a Colossus. But she is a giant with feet of clay. There is as much of a chance that she will implode and drag her trading partners down into the abyss with her as there is that she will embark on overseas military adventures. China's internal problems are too great to allow her the luxury of overseas campaigns. China cannot be Asia's lodestar for the new millennium. Her GDP per head is simply too small to fuel sustained international growth. China's bankrupt banks, her corrupt and inefficient state enterprises, and her massive 100 million strong army of unemployed workers all create their own imperial imperative to expand into neighboring lands, Taiwan and Russia's Far East being the most obvious, but not the only, targets. All of these demographic and economic social pressures will make China a particularly volatile force to be reckoned with in the years to come. The Chinese Communist Party has the world's biggest human resource management problem. It must keep the Middle Kingdom intact and stop her disintegrating. That is no easy task.

China's economy is rife with all the conditions that caused crises in other Asian countries. These include massive crony capitalism, bad bank loans that dwarf those of any other Asian nation, and very inefficient capital allocation procedures. China's second largest financial trust company, the Guangdong International Trust and Investment Corporation, failed in 1999. Because many others totter on the verge of failure, a total collapse in China is a distinct possibility. China's fixation with huge and risky projects only reinforces this scenario. By far the biggest of all China's current gargantuan projects is the Three Gorges dam project on the Yangtze River. Completed in 2009, the dam is far and away the world's largest concrete structure. It is 650 feet high, more than two miles wide, and it has created a reservoir more than 400 miles long. It consumes more material than all of Egypt's pyramids and and it has cost over $70 billion. Its hydroelectric generator produces the equivalent of 15 giant nuclear reactors. If it fails, it will lead to increased turmoil in an already unstable country.

China's development policies are in marked contrast to those of Taiwan. Whereas Taiwan has preferred to diversify its interests and to allow a myriad of small companies to be the dynamo for growth, China has preferred to go for broke. The type of large projects that the Three Gorges dam typifies could bring China down. China's development eggs are in too few baskets. The collapse of any of her giant projects could bring the whole society tumbling down as well.

China is still taking too many giant leaps forward. Chinese leaders are performing a high wire act, which makes only one thing certain. Whether China achieves economic lift-off or whether China implodes, China will be a very frustrated and awkward customer to deal with. Territorial conquests will whet the appetite for more of the same. Economic collapse will lead to calls for diversionary military moves against Taiwan—and Japan. China is a giant jewel that must be carefully embedded into the international community. For a variety of historical reasons, this too is no easy task.

The Chinese government must preserve national unity at all costs. And, if economic collapse happens, there is always the recourse to patriotism. And Japan, the former colonial master, makes a big and unifying target. China already claims the Japanese held Senkaku Islands between Okinawa and Taiwan for herself. Mirroring her claims to the Spratly Islands, China claims that the Senkaku Islands have been indisputably Chinese from as early as 1372! Beijing claims that Japan has been a mere interloper there. As the victor in the 1894–95 war with China, Japan seized these islands along with Taiwan and the Penghu Islands and incorporated them into Okinawa Prefecture as Japanese territory. China is now trying to prise them back. Mirroring her war of nerves against Taiwan, China has conducted missile tests in the waters off the Senkaku Islands and, unless Japan asserts herself, she will most likely regularize this tactic over time as well. China lodges strong diplomatic objections any time Japanese officials visit the islands and her military research vessels continue to encroach on Japanese waters around the islands. The Senkaku Islands is, in other words, another Spratly Islands or Taiwan in the making. If Japan wishes to retain sovereignty of these islands, she will need more than a checkbook. She will need a strong navy and a diplomatic offensive to deter China. Of the of 1,992 ship incursions into Japanese waters during 1999, the overwhelming majority, 1,547, were Chinese. Even more so than North Korea, China is continuing to probe unimpeded into Japan's maritime defenses.

Japan's policy is to keep her head buried in the sand and to hope that things will settle down once again. China has other ideas. She says that Japan's claims are based on its victory in the 1894–95 war and that its defeat in the Pacific War negated those claims. Like all of China's other territorial claims, there are some gaping holes that Japan's diplomats should be alluding to. The Cairo Declaration jointly issued by China, the United States and

Britain during World War II stipulated the return to China by Japan of all the territory she had annexed during and after the 1894–95 war. The PRC claims that forfeiture of these islands were implicitly included in Japan's surrender; they were not explicitly included. China argues that the Cairo Declaration and the Potsdam Proclamation, which affirmed it, make these islands Chinese. The Chinese claim Kume Island to be the beginning of Japan's Ryukyu territory and of Okinawa Prefecture; the rest of the islands, Beijing claims, are theirs alone. China claims that, prior to the 1894–95 war, the entire Ryukyu Islands paid tribute to China and were therefore Chinese. China, in other words, claims all the islands between Taiwan and Okinawa as Chinese and says that Okinawa is probably Chinese as well.

China's claims over the Senkaku Islands should not be dismissed out of hand. These islands have considerable emotional appeal to Beijing's leaders. China sees the capture of these islands by Japan's imperial forces at the end of the nineteenth century as heralding her own fall and Japan's consequent rise. The annexation of these islands was indeed the beginning of the Japanese empire—and of today's enmity between Japan and China. After the Tenno government forcibly carried out the Ryukyu Disposal and incorporated the islands into the Okinawa Prefecture, Japan then forced Korea to sign a treaty and open its ports for trading. This paved the way for Korea's annexation, Japan's rise to power and China's consequent demise.

The War of JiaWu began in July 1894 between China and Japan to achieve hegemony on the Korean peninsula. The war ended with the parties signing the Treaty of MaKwan (Shimonoseki) on April 17, 1895. Defeated, China was forced to pay a huge indemnity of some 350 million yen. Because this large sum dwarfed the then Japanese national annual income of 80 million yen, it allowed Japan to achieve economic lift-off. China's silver and gold was used to boost Japan and further cripple China. The Senkaku Islands' defeat fueled Imperial Japan's overseas adventures and helped emasculate China at the same time. This is not something China can lightly forget. It was as integral to China's century of shame as were the Opium Wars, themselves a terrible indictment of the rape of China by foreign imperial powers.

Although even in defeat, China could still claim the nebulous power of her ancient culture, this victory put Japan well on the road to achieving the hard power of military and economic force, which were the international currencies of the day. Japan's decisive victory effectively destroyed China's hopes of hegemony not only in Korea, but also in the entire region and thereby shaped the futures of both countries up to August 1945. Although history could conceivably have been different, Japan's better organization set the parameters on the march of both nations over the next half-century.

Peace meant that China had to surrender the Liaotung Peninsula, Taiwan, and the Pescadores to Japan. Liaotung cemented Japan's hold on Korea and Taiwan provided strategic bases for the Japanese navy. Taken together, they gave Japan the scope for its further expansions, which only further weakened China. This process continued until the wholesale eruptions, which followed the 1937 Marco Polo Bridge incident and ignited the eight-year war between the two nations. The eight years which followed further deepened China's hatred of Japanese involvement on Asia's mainland.

Whereas the 1894–95 war weakened China considerably, it had the opposite effect on Japan. China's massive reparations paid for the Yawata Iron Works, the first modern factory built during the Meiji era. This was the basis for Japan's considerable armaments industry. Japan also built a modern railway structure, which further served to unify the country. China didn't and paid the price in military terms.

Though both adopted the "rich country, strong army" slogan at the end of the nineteenth century, only Japan turned the rhetoric into reality. Japan increasingly dominated China economically. It accounted for almost 40 percent of its trade deficit. Japan's China conquests also allowed it to emerge as a world power, which the European powers had to respect. The European powers abandoned their unequal and unenforceable treaties with Japan and allowed her access to their markets. China, by contrast, continued to be ravaged. The Great Powers, with Japan playing an increasingly large part, continued to milk China dry until the end of the Great War, when Japan and the United States were left with the field almost entirely to themselves. Japan, much more so than the United States, continued to suck China dry.

The August 1945 surrender should have spelt the end of Japanese power and the consequent rise of China. However, the Chinese civil war intervened. Japan was swallowed whole into the American camp and, following the Communist takeover, China latched itself on to the Soviet camp. Still, old enmities continued to flicker and, from the Chinese side, to have their considerable advantages. When Japan sent minesweepers to Korea to assist the American war effort, China used it as an excuse to invade. They insisted that the units they sent across the Yalu in 1950 were to check the revival in Japanese militarism, which the minesweepers exemplified. China used Japan's token contribution to the Korean War as a propaganda weapon to unleash her own forces and to polarize world opinion by setting the entire Korean peninsula ablaze. If nothing else, the carnage which followed showed the depth of China's hatred for its former colonial master.

Japan's historical exploitation of China is a running sore, which Beijing cannot forget or forgive. Japan, by any stretch of the imagination, was not a kind imperial master. Japan's Manchurian adventure is, in fact, like a casebook from hell. Shiro Ishii, a world-class bacteriologist, founded unit 731 in a remote, high security Japanese Army camp in occupied Manchuria. Ishii's aim was to develop, irrespective of moral and legal considerations, a biological weapons capability that would win China for Emperor Hirohito—and for Japan. Ishii exposed his Chinese prisoners to plague, anthrax and mustard gas, as well as extremes of scorching heat and freezing cold—and debased all of humanity in the process.

Sheldon Harris' 1994 book, *Factories of Death*, details how Ishii's Japanese medical units carried out their germ warfare experiments on humans, how they infected both American prisoners and Chinese civilians with plague and anthrax; how they performed amputations to train medical students, often without anesthesia; and how they conducted frostbite experiments where they exposed various parts of the body to minus 40-degree temperatures, before attempting to defrost them. These Japanese doctors carved up their patients, without even the fig leaf of an anesthetic and dissected them until their remains were so small that they had to be scraped off the operating tables. These good doctors experimented on children; even three-day-old babies were tortured in their scientific experiments. Men were staked to the ground and biological weapons were used on them to see how slowly they would die. Inhuman as all of these experiments were, they had immediate practical relevance. By the war's end, the Japanese had exploded over 2,000 Uji chemical and biological warfare (CBW) bombs and had also tested the more lethal Ha CBW bomb as well. The fatality rates rarely fell below 70 percent and, given time, would have reached 100 percent. Chinese fatalities from Unit 731's war are inestimable. Flasks containing cholera, dysentery, typhoid, plague, anthrax, and para-typhoid germs were dumped into reservoirs, wells, and rivers. So comprehensive was this CBW campaign that Japanese units who overran infected Chinese positions suffered catastrophic losses themselves: over 10,000 in a single attack on the No-an suburb of Hsinking in 1942.

Ishii planned to breed 300 kg, approximately one billion plague fleas, for the ultimate battle in defense of Hirohito. So successful was Unit 731's conveyor belt system that, by spring 1945, they had sufficient plague, typhoid, cholera and anthrax organisms to kill half the planet. Imperial Japan had, to repeat, plans to kill half the planet and they only aborted those plans after the American attacks on Nagasaki and Hiroshima convinced Hirohito and his closest cronies that the game was up.

Much as the Japanese government and their collaborators would like to forget it, Unit 731's crimes against humanity continue. Chinese citizens are still dying from the chemical weapons Hirohito's henchmen unleashed on them. Many of them have sued. Japan's sanctimonious, parsimonious and hypocritical position on financial compensation is that the issue was settled in the 1951 San Francisco Peace Treaty. In that treaty, Japan agreed to surrender unconditionally and the Allies agreed not to bring any more Japanese war criminals to justice. Japan's refusal to compensate its victims directly for the atrocities is partly due to the lack of pressure from other countries, especially the United States and China. The United States preferred a stable ally as well as Unit 731's secrets to implementing justice. The Chinese forsook their right to compensation for economic aid and for morally and politically blackmailing their former adversaries.

Japan's record is as blemished as Nazi Germany's. Nanking, during the six weeks that began on December 13, 1937, witnessed some of the worst acts of barbarism ever recorded. Japanese soldiers under the direct command of Prince Asaka Yasuhiko, the uncle of Japanese Emperor Hirohito, committed unprecedented levels of rape, plunder and pillage. Thousands of civilians were buried or burned alive, or used as targets for bayonet practice. They were gunned down in large groups and tossed like so much garbage into the Yangtze River. Even that level of debauchery did not satisfy these Japanese soldiers, who were working under strict orders at all times. Many soldiers went beyond rape to disembowel women, slice off their breasts or nail them to walls. Fathers were forced to rape their daughters, and sons their mothers, as other family members were made to watch. Not only did live burials, public castrations and the roasting alive of prisoners become routine, but other, equally diabolical variations were visited on the Chinese military and civilians alike. Prisoners were hanged by their tongues on iron hooks or buried waist-deep to be then savaged into pieces by ravenous dogs.

Although Japan continues to deny that anything untoward took place during those six weeks, the international community estimates that more than 300,000 Chinese were killed, and at least 10,000 women were systematically raped. This is an extraordinary figure for a city with a population of only 650,000 and easily outpaces most of the Nazis' atrocities. It is a well-documented atrocity that Japan must own-up in full to. Japan's refusal to admit its crimes can largely be explained by their leaders' total lack of a moral, human conscience. The shabby way these self-same, self-serving politicians have treated their wartime comfort women and their other war-slaves remains a running sore which still poisons relationships between Japan and the countries they press-ganged their sex slaves from.

The comfort women were mostly Koreans and Chinese teenagers and, as such, were at the lower end of the Japanese empire's value system spectrum. Japan's comfort women were press-ganged into the slave trade by the Japanese Imperial Army during the Pacific War. These children were confined in "comfort stations" throughout occupied Asia, where Japanese soldiers systematically gang-raped them. Analogous to the POWs who were labeled as blocks of wood, the comfort women were classified as military supplies and were shipped from battlefront to mining camp to factory town, enduring years of brutal sexual servitude to Hirohito's foot-soldiers. Up to 200,000 women, among them Chinese, Indonesian, Dutch and Filipinas as well as Koreans, were forced into sexual slavery in Japanese military brothels. Of these 200,000 sex slaves, only 40,000 lived through the ordeal. Less than 500 are believed to be still alive today. Of the estimated 200,000 women who were conscripted, perhaps 75 percent died during the war by venereal disease, tuberculosis, violence, and suicide. The others survived to live out wrecked shadows of lives in a society that despised them as "unclean." Theirs is a horrific story, only recently made public after a half-century of Japanese-induced silence and shame. Theirs is a story that Japan must eventually face up to if Tokyo is ever to enjoy normal relations with her neighbors.

For all of these reasons, Japan's rapacious Imperial Army is still contentious in China and Korea. Infected as they were with the racist-tinged doctrines of Charles Darwin, Julian Huxley, and Herbert Spencer, they inflicted unimaginable cruelties on the countries they overran, Korea and China in particular. Japan has yet to pay substantial reparations. She has yet to admit the full extent of her perfidies and hopes against hope that the moral tempest will pass. This will not happen until Japan comes clean.

Although plain common sense would say that Japan should admit her past wrongs and face the consequences, her neighbors have been kept waiting a very long time. Japan did not admit their wartime sex slave program even existed until 1994, two years after the first of the women stepped forward. Not only did they not admit their perfidies but Japanese leaders were openly contemptuous of their victims. Seisuke Okuno, a former education minister and a member of the ruling Liberal Democrat Party, claims, in a popular political refrain, that the comfort women were willing volunteers. Another coalition MP, Tadashi Itagaki, had the gall to call Ms Kim Sang Hee, a former Korean sex slave fighting for compensation, a liar, who submitted herself to continual rape in the comfort stations for money.

International opinion does not agree with these unadulterated fascists. An International Labor Organization panel of experts in March 1996 ruled that Japan's war-time use of comfort women should be characterized as sexual slavery, a violation of the ILO's 1930 Forced Labor Convention. The United Nations Commission on Human Rights called on Japan to pay compensation to the surviving World War II sex slaves. The International Commission of Jurists ruled in November 1994 that "It is indisputable that these women were forced, deceived, coerced, and abducted to provide sexual services to the Japanese military ... [Japan] violated customary norms of international law concerning war crimes, crimes against humanity, slavery and the trafficking in women and children … Japan should take full responsibility now, and make suitable restitution to the victims and their families."

The UN Human Rights Commission declared in 1996 that the Japanese government should assume state responsibility and acknowledge its violation of international law and moral decency; make a public apology in writing and pay hefty compensation to the individual women who still survive; reform their educational curricula to admit the horrible truth of these incidents; release all relevant documents they still possess; and, lastly, identify and punish the perpetrators. Fat chance!

China will remain justly suspicious of Japan until Japan apologizes and makes amends. They see all Japanese attempts at engagement as a form of attempted moral bribery. Like their North Korean counterparts, China's leaders see Japan's Sunshine engagement policies as an attempt to infuse them with emasculating economic, cultural, and ideological influences. They see engagement, containment and TMD as merely flip sides of this same warped coin. China does not want to be either contained or ensnared any more. China instead wishes to resume her historical Middle Kingdom role, with Korea, Japan and her other neighbors being pushed to the margins. To achieve this end, she wishes above all else to handle her internal and external economic and related challenges in such a manner that both Communist rule and China's unity are further entrenched and enhanced. Beijing's human rights policies, its foreign arms and dual-technology sales, and its militarized diplomacy in the South China Sea—and, eventually, in the Senkaku Islands—must all be seen in this light. So too must its military travails on the historic margins of its empire. Beijing's brutal consolidation of Tibet and Xinjiang and its war of nerves against Taiwan are all manifestations of the same imperative. So too is its reaffirmation of sovereignty over the Senkaku Islands. All of these consolidate Communist rule and reinforce the country's centralizing tendencies. All of them mean that China deserves serious consideration.

Although China might well be Asia's Middle Kingdom, the satellite nations will have to determine how they should interact with her. As well as TMD, this will entail closer economic and diplomatic cooperation between the United States, South Korea, Japan, Indonesia, Myanmar, Russia, Vietnam, and India. China, of course, will not sit idly by and allow itself to be encircled. It will continue to court and arm Pakistan and the rogue nations of the Middle East to break out of any such encirclement. The idea of holding Russia, Vietnam, India, and Japan in the one stable alliance presents its own formidable problems, ones that China would most likely exploit. Crucially, however, in all this, Japan must play a role. She can no longer slavishly rely on the United States. Instead, she will have to chart her way through Asia's increasingly choppy waters to get the right balance that maintains peace and stability in the region. No matter what path she should embark on, this will involve a much more sophisticated diplomatic and military strategy by Japan.

Because containment presents its obvious problems, engagement has its attractions. Proponents of this policy would argue that China is best when it is included in the decision-making process. They would say that China has proved an exemplary member of institutions such as the IMF and World Bank and that it always pays its debts on time. China's sheer size means that it has to be engaged. Its implosion would set back the whole of Asia by at least a generation.

Although China's policies can be easily painted as those of a pragmatic if somewhat greedy realist, this is a superficial view. The skeptics point out that Beijing's leaders aim to derive the maximum benefits they can from the global institutions they are involved in, while simultaneously minimizing their obligations. These people point to China's Permanent Council seat in the United Nations as a case in point. China has 20 percent of the UN's permanent veto power but pays less than one percent of its budget.

That power is a very good return for their money. Although, the issue of recognizing Taiwan apart, China has been slow to use her veto power, she has been extremely recalcitrant in other forums. She regularly withholds compliance on agreements of high value to the outside world to extract benefits in return on issues like Taiwan and the attacks on her human rights record, issues that she feels particularly strongly about. In this, she merely mirrors the United States in trying to arrange matters to suit herself. Countries that want access to China's markets have to turn a blind eye to her gulag economy. The notorious Laogai prison system holds between six and eight million Chinese citizens captive and employed in over 140 slave-labor industries that ship to more than 70 countries around the world. Japan and other countries wishing to operate in the PRC must ignore these abuses—and the long-term ramifications to themselves.

However, it is naïve to expect Western standards of comfort in such a poverty-racked nation. Simply managing China, simply keeping her from falling apart, is a gargantuan job in itself. China would see its efforts at achieving economic lift-off as an attempt to help all of its citizens through the trickle down effect. Small comfort to her political prisoners but given the sheer size of her population, her leaders would argue that it is the only realistic path to take. Western forms of democracy, they would argue, are just too divisive and expensive a luxury to entertain. This is a viewpoint, which has wide resonance throughout Asia. Although Singapore, for example, might be more restrictive than many Western European countries, it is a magnet of opportunity for millions of Asians, who would gladly do anything within their power to land a visa to work there.

Singapore is only a tiny city-state. China is a giant, faced not only with an array of every conceivable kind of economic, military and political problem imaginable but with the anarchy of the former Soviet Union and Indonesia to remind it of the consequences of failure. China therefore has little to gain from listening to cliché-studded lectures. She demands a more sophisticated approach, one that Japan has yet to really develop.

Only a process of engagement can bring China's considerable failings to prominence in a proactive way. The actions of China's Khmer Rouge allies, who killed 3,500,000 fellow-Cambodians by hunger, hunger-related diseases and summary executions in their Gulag Cambodienne, exemplify this point. There is little point now in harping on the historical fact that the Khmer Rouge could not have operated without the active support of the PRC or that the Western powers periodically used these thugs to counteract Vietnam, or that China's main regional enemy, Vietnam, toppled them. Therefore, just as Japan has a historical debt to pay to Korea and China, so also has the PRC an equally large debt to pay to Cambodia. Japan should tie its reparations payments to issues such as this so that a better Asia may eventually emerge from the savagery its people have all endured. Once Japan admits the past, she too can play the human rights card to the benefit of all. There is little to be gained in using these sufferings as a political sledgehammer. Japanese money can talk louder.

But that can only be done by a process of engagement. Once Japan embarks on such a course of action, China will have to see the considerable wrongs she has suffered in their wider perspective. Once China can be engaged in such dialog, then she can be confronted on the issue of arms proliferation as well. Although China sells only about a tenth of the weaponry on the international markets the United States does, she sells them to some pretty obnoxious customers. Around 95 percent of China's arms exports are delivered to immediate neighbors or to the Middle East. These markets include Pakistan, Afghanistan, Iran, Iraq, Sudan, and North Korea, all of which are real or potential enemies of the West. Although the 1992 Gore-McCain Act prescribed sanctions for the sale of advanced conventional weapons by any nation to Iran, the PRC has transferred at least 60 C-802 cruise missiles to Iran, and has therefore put the entire U.S. Navy's Fifth Fleet at risk. The CIA has designated the People's Republic of China the most significant supplier of weapons of mass destruction (WMD) related goods and technology to America's enemies. China is the most active supplier of Iran's chemical, nuclear, and biological weapons program. Because China cannot be meaningfully punished for these transgressions, she must be proactively engaged.

China, in other words, must be diplomatically engaged about TMD as well as any proposed Japanese military build up and both of these can be linked to her own defense budgets. Although China has legitimate concerns about a Japanese build-up, she must realize that Japan has reasons to fear her own numerous legions. As well as having the world's largest standing army, China not only uses her own arms in anger but also proliferates them to some of the world's most bellicose countries. Beijing must realize that her awesome might has to be of concern to Japan. Because Japan has not fired a shot in anger in over fifty years, she can therefore lecture Beijing—once she makes amends for the vile sins of the past.

The sooner this starts the better for everybody. China is using the cash windfall of its $40 billion a year trade advantage to build an even more fearsome military arsenal. The Chinese shopping list includes several aircraft carriers, modern missile-equipped warships, nuclear attack submarines, fighter aircraft, and land-based intercontinental ballistic missiles with multiple warheads. Given China's exercises in the Taiwan Strait and her claims over Japanese territory, all of this gives Japan reasons to ponder, if not to unilaterally rearm.

Although Japan can instead issue protests through G8 and the like, China's money speaks louder. Russia and Israel have teamed up to build China an AWACS system, using Israel's Phalcon radar. Israel has given Beijing the Patriot missile's classified technology. Israel has also used U.S. technology incorporated into its own Lavi plane to build China's next fighter aircraft—the J-10—complete with airborne radar systems, tank programs and a variety of missiles. Israel's transfer to China of its STAR-1 cruise missile technology gives China an insight into America's stealth bomber technology—a handy bit of knowledge should the engagement process fail. Israel has also transferred to China the most lethal air-to-air missile in the world: the Python 4. This system employs an advanced helmet-mounted sight, developed together by American and Israeli firms for use against potential enemies such as the PRC!

Moscow has sold China 48 SU-27 fighters with a licensing deal for 200 more and is planning to sell them the SU-30. Russia is also producing for China 30 Sunburn anti-ship missiles that skim the ocean's surface at twice the speed of sound. China has recently bought 50 SU-27 ground attack fighters from Russia and it will assemble another 150 herself. This all-weather jet also fires air-to-air missiles more accurately than any other non-American fighter does. These supersonic babies will make China a very real force to contend with, not only in the skies over the Taiwan Strait, but in the entire South China Sea as well.

China has also bought four Kilo-636 attack submarines from Russia. These submarines will end the hegemony the U.S. Seventh Fleet currently enjoys around Asian waters. Although most of China's arms imports come from Russia, France has also secured significant orders. France is allowing China to produce the Z-9a Red Thunder jet helicopter under license. These choppers will come in useful for such handy little jobs as dropping commandos into Taiwan and dropping anti-submarine weapons into Taiwanese waters, as well as other waters in the South and East China Seas.

All in all, China is spending an impressive $11 billion a year on such purposes. Although it will be several years yet before the Chinese can match the Americans in firepower, it won't be for the lack of trying. They are already tilting the balance of power away from the United States in the East Asian theater. America, remember, always has the option of sailing back home across the Pacific. Japan will be stuck with the consequences unless her diplomatic and military leaders make counter-plans now.

Although China has developed and bought an impressive range

of hardware, it still lacks key components before it becomes a truly world class military power. It must, for example, develop the information technology capability to coordinate air, land, and sea forces. This and other logistical bottlenecks will be cleared in time. China is turning out engineering and science graduates in much bigger numbers than either Japan or the United States. Although proponents of engagement would argue that China's vast projects need these equally vast infusions of skilled personnel, there is another side to the story. In military science, it is the absolute number of scientists, not the proportionate amount in the population, which is important. That is one reason why North Korea can have a world class military and a starving population at the same time: Pyongyang puts its engineering expertise into guns, not butter. Because China can do this to a much greater degree, her military potential is all the greater. Further, because China's vast reservoir of trained scientists continues to grow in absolute numbers, so too does her military potential.

So, too, does China's industrialization policy, which differs from Japan's post-war policies of technology transfer in only one crucial aspect. China can use the technology for military purposes. Although all foreign high technology firms investing in the Chinese market are under sustained pressure to transfer commercial technologies and know-how as a condition of market access and investment approval in the People's Republic of China, American and Japanese companies are under particular pressure to do so. These technology transfer packages are explicitly mandated in the regulations and industrial policies of the PRC and, generally speaking, unless tendering firms offer substantial technology transfer sweeteners, they lose out to their more accommodating competitors. Although the technologies sought by the Chinese authorities are not usually directly related to the security field, their cumulative effects raise her technological prowess to a degree that will allow her to undermine the West's military supremacy. Thus, the prospect of exporting civilian technology to Beijing has long-term national security risks attached to it. The cumulative effect of such business practices is to increase China's military and economic potential in the entire region.

China's policy of playing competing firms off against each other reinforces this trend. China's tariff and non-tariff trade barriers, as well as its stated desire to develop indigenous industries, make gains from investment difficult to realize unless the investing firms give China the technological know-how and know-why she craves. In addition, foreign investors, who are not on the inside track, often find artificial barriers to selling their particular products in the Chinese market. Often, the only way these non-Chinese companies can gain a foothold in the Chinese marketplace is through joint ventures with Chinese firms. Generally speaking, the host company tends to hijack the technology and use it to compete against the foreign company both in China and beyond the Middle Kingdom as well.

This was Du Pont's experience. They formed a joint alliance with a government-backed company, who took their technology, relabeled it and used it to try to force them out of not only Chinese markets, but all of Asia. Du Pont's dilemma is part of a wider one. Because of the huge potential China's markets hold, they stayed, these thefts of their intellectual property notwithstanding. As the Du Pont case exemplifies, the massive size of China's market makes it extremely difficult for Japanese and other foreign companies to ignore its commercial potential. The establishment of technology development facilities by successful foreign companies is often the key to keeping out other foreign competitors. As long as China is demanding technology transfers as a condition of doing business, and other countries are encouraging—and in some cases actively participating in—technology transfer schemes with Chinese entities, Chinese leverage in dealings with Japanese companies is enormous.

China, like Mother Nature herself, abhors a vacuum. China will be able to fill whatever vacuums the diminution of American forces in Asia gives rise to. Although she is making great economic strides, she is taking great risks in her efforts to modernize. China's vast population is getting used to rising standards of living. Beijing will have to meet these even if the country slides into prolonged recession. Territorial expansion—a hot war—could either allow the people's expectations to be fulfilled, or at least divert them long enough to allow Beijing's leadership survive until the next crisis sets in. Japan must prepare for these contingencies by clearing the hurdles of history in the first instance and being able to meet any military challenges afterwards.

The Chinese dragon, asleep for so long, is now awakening and, as Napoleon correctly predicted, is giving the world cause to ponder and to tremble. China has the capacity to be a very big, intractable and almost invincible power. The road China eventually travels will dictate the road her neighbors will have to trek as well. Given the giant leaps into the dark the Chinese economy is making, that road is far from clear. Whether China emerges as a highly aggressive great power, or whether it evolves into a powerful country following a reasonable foreign policy of constructive engagement with the rest of the world or whether it eventually implodes, will shape the future of the entire world, Japan included. The PRC is, after all, undergoing its greatest political changes since the 1949 Communist victory in the Chinese Civil War and the type of country that will emerge from all this turmoil is not at all fully certain. China simply faces too many challenges to say for sure what she will look like in the decades ahead.

These challenges focus on China's abandonment of centralized Maoism and its adoption of capitalism and the decentralization and pluralism of power, which capitalism entails. Because the PLA is central to all of these changes, there is a high likelihood that China will follow Russia and Indonesia into anarchy. The PLA's fighting force capabilities were seriously degraded in recent years by its many lucrative business ventures, which were a distraction from its primary military mission of defending and upholding

China's national integrity. Despite its lucrative business distractions, the PLA remains hugely nationalistic and is one of the most important unifying forces in the nation. The danger is that Beijing might use nationalistic expansionism to keep its vast nation welded together. Its ideology discredited, the moral authority of the Communist Party has been seriously eroded. Meanwhile, nascent capitalism is causing a plurality of moral and financial power to develop and, as a consequence, Beijing is being deprived of one of its major levers of control over the provinces.

Lacking the ability to extract sufficient revenues from the richer provinces, Beijing is also losing control over the poorer inland provinces. It can no longer supply them with the services necessary to command their loyalty. The central government has founded a new paramilitary organization, the People's Armed Police (PAP), to maintain order, but Beijing's shortage of funds has made it difficult to sustain this force. Moreover, government bureaucrats and the police cannot survive on the low salaries paid by Beijing and are increasingly relying on extortion and other corrupt practices to support and enrich themselves at the people's expense. This has further discredited the central government, especially in the poor inland provinces, where the inhabitants cannot pay the bribes the local government officials and forces of law and order demand.

Meanwhile, the richer provinces are traversing along a different road. They are busily expanding their overseas commercial contacts, securing their own oil supplies and, in the process, building regional governments that are autonomous in everything but name. Most notably, wealthy Guangdong with its 65 million people and an extraordinary annual GNP growth of 20 percent now enjoys considerable autonomy from Beijing. These coastal regions are enjoying the lion's share of the foreign investment that has flowed into China in recent years.

The overseas Chinese communities, which Beijing has largely ignored up to now, have been responsible for much of this inward investment. The overseas Chinese, largely descended from immigrants from the coastal provinces, have in many cases retained strong regional loyalties. The 50–60 million overseas Chinese are estimated to control up to $2 trillion in assets, a significant portion of which has flowed back into the coastal provinces over the past 15 years. This largesse helps to explain the huge boom in the economy of eastern China; this large investment has also increased provincial independence from Beijing's control. Taiwan has also played a major role in these developments for reasons that Beijing is justly suspicious of. Japan has been pursuing a broadly similar path in the northern coastal provinces. But whether or not these developments will subvert Beijing's authority or not remains highly uncertain. Political power in China is more likely to come out of the barrel of a PLA gun than a Japanese or Taiwanese checkbook. Certainly, none of these investors should be under any illusions about Beijing's determination to use the gun. The daunting task of holding a quarter of the world's population under one government would give anyone an itchy trigger finger. There are just too many things that can go wrong.

In contrast to the population of the coastal provinces, the 100 million non-Han Chinese national minorities within the PRC now present little danger to the unity of the country. Although Tibet continues to harbor the strongest nationalist movement, the 2 million Tibetans still living in their homeland are no match for the local PLA garrison. The different ethnic groups in Xinjiang have been more restive since the disintegration of the Soviet Union and the independence of the Central Asian Republics; however, their violence has been contained by the PLA and the PAP as well as China's oil diplomacy in central Asia. Thus, although these regions are now quiescent, they could turn violent if the rest of China were to erupt. In other words, if the center were to lose enough control over the provinces in some future power struggle, Tibet and Xinjiang might copy recent examples in the dying days of the Soviet Union and make a bid to break away from the PRC.

As if that was not enough, Beijing has other territorial headaches to occupy herself with. In addition to her territorial claims over the Spratly Islands and Taiwan, Beijing also claims parts of Kazakhstan, Tajikistan, Kirgizstan, and Siberia. Already, the growth in the Chinese economy is exerting a powerful attraction on the ex-Soviet territories along the Chinese border. Illegal Chinese emigration into Siberia and the Russian Far East is also considerable. Previous Russian fears about Japanese designs on Siberia have been replaced by worries about Chinese intentions toward that gigantic, resource-rich but under-populated region. These disputes will also ultimately involve Japan.

The Russian Far East is, in other words, another flash point that Japan must worry about. Although the regional demographic imperative favors China, Russia cannot allow itself to be colonized by default. She needs to be able to resist this pressure. Only a Russian-Japanese entente can keep the Russian Far East out of China's hands. The region is broke and, currently, the only dynamic vehicle in the area is China. Russia's difficulty is Japan's opportunity. Japan should increase its investments in the region. Sakhalin Island in the Russian Far East is just 40 km north of Japan and is surrounded by the Sea of Okhotsk, the Sea of Japan, and the Pacific Ocean. The large, isolated island has only 650,000 people, who mostly eke out a living from the marine fishing industry. Recent oil discoveries are changing this. The Sakhalin II project, for example, a US$10 billion offshore oil project, targets the Piltun-Astokhskoye offshore oil-gas field of the northeast coast. Its recoverable reserves are estimated at 750 million barrels of crude oil and 14 trillion cubic feet of natural gas. Mitsui, Mitsubishi, and the Japan Export Import Bank (JEXIM) are among its major funders. JEXIM, for example, has provided US$116 million, and it is also financing the first stage of crude oil production.

Russia's Far East needs these Japanese funds to fend off China's challenge. Russia is nearly bankrupt and its puny national finances rank with those of the Netherlands and other minnow powers. The economies of East Siberia, the Far East, and the Far North, which were formerly given support for military and related non-economic considerations, are in dire straits. There is no other way in the long term for these regions, forsaken by European Russia, to survive economically than to engage in economic exchanges with either China or Japan. Whereas Japan does not really need these Russian outposts, they need Japan. If the Northern Territories issue can be resolved, and if the two countries agree to mutual economic and military cooperation, then Japan will have achieved a lot. She will have succeeded in securing her northern borders that have been problematic since the end of the Edo Period. More importantly, she will have also expanded her range of foreign policy options. She will be in a position to deflate the threat China poses by forming alliances with the other major regional powers. This will be crucial as China's teething problems come to bear on the region's balance of power. Japan needs a confident Russia to balance China.

As nationalism has increasingly replaced communism as the Chinese government's ideology, there have been signs of a regression by some Chinese officials to the Middle Kingdom's ancient attitudes of superiority to its neighbors. If these attitudes become widespread among Chinese leaders, the Chinese could be expected to firmly oppose Indian and Japanese efforts to obtain permanent UN Security Council seats. Indeed, India's quest for a permanent UN seat could be expected to be linked with Japan's and, via Pakistan, to find China exercising her veto on both countries. Further, Chinese attempts to ring its abundant borders with a band of friendly states for defensive reasons might be interpreted in New Delhi, Moscow, and Tokyo as creating spheres of influence at Indian, Russian, or Japanese expense. A Japanese entente with Russia would do a lot to build long term bridges with Beijing as well. Japan must try to engage in jaw-jaw as opposed to war-war. China's demographics dictate that.

Japan's population is aging and shrinking whereas China's is still youthful. As a result, China outnumbers Japan in military-age manpower by a ratio of fifteen to one. This has immense tactical repercussions. Given its high density of population in Tokyo and a handful of other urban areas, Japan is extremely vulnerable to nuclear attack. As few as three or four thermonuclear explosions would totally devastate Japan's capacity to function. To inflict equivalent damage on Russia or China, Japan would need to hit back with 100 or more warheads. Because she lacks strategic depth and possesses a long and very vulnerable coastline, Japan is almost as vulnerable against conventional attack. Japan has also very exposed sea corridors linking it to its vital supplies in such distant places as the Middle East.

Japan has a glass jaw, one that China could easily break if Japan does not act responsibly over the next few years. If China is not to deliver a knockout blow, Japan must not only rearm but must take the diplomatic initiative in the region as well. Because Japan does not have any formal regional military alliances, she must develop closer ties with the ASEAN states, Thailand, Vietnam, and Indonesia in particular. Japan must also use her existing economic links with Australia to develop closer military ones. The same is true, of course, with South Korea and Taiwan. As long as Japan keeps the military alliance with America in order, and as long as she does nothing to unduly provoke China, all of these actions will go to make Japan and the entire region more stable.

Japan's ultimate objective must be one of presenting China with the very real prospect of encirclement by a Japanese financed alliance, which would include Indonesia, India, Russia, and Japan and have such satellite countries as Australia as minor partners. Such an alliance would match China numerically, would overwhelm it technologically and would guarantee the freedom of the region's sea-lanes. Ultimately, it would therefore improve the well being of the entire region, China included. Although other strategies are possible, China must be engaged within very strict and predictable parameters. Although the primary effort must be diplomatic, the Japanese defense forces must be unleashed as well.

JAPAN:
The Toothless Tiger

Japan is the only major nation in the world that has explicitly renounced war as a tool of policy. Article 9.1 of the Japanese constitution renounces war "as a sovereign right of the nation." Article 9.2 asserts that "land, sea and air forces, as well as other war potential, will never be maintained."

That said, Japan maintains very substantial "land, sea and air forces." Japan's military expenditures are, in fact, the third highest in the world. Japan has the capacity to pack a punch. Although the Japanese tiger still hides behind America's apron strings, it could very quickly develop its own awesome fangs. If Japan wants a permanent United Nations Security Council seat, it must emulate the United States, Britain, France, Russia, and China. It must develop its fighting forces and run the inevitable gauntlet of protests from the PRC and its other former colonies. If Japan remains a toothless tiger, she might end up witnessing China subsuming Taiwan and North Korea continuing to use Japan as a firing range for its missiles. Japan must choose between packing a punch and remaining militarily defanged and emasculated.

Because China will not stand idly by and watch its former colonial ruler rearm, Japan must launch a diplomatic offensive to explain its needs. Tokyo must also ensure its neighbors, Korea and China in particular, that the days of military adventurism are long over. Although in an ideal world, this would be an easy task, Japan's imperial history makes it more daunting.

Because Japan's formal processes for coordination between the Japanese Foreign Ministry and the Japan Defense Agency is broadly based and well institutionalized, there is little chance of remilitarization by the back door. The chances for autonomous military action by Japan's defense forces are presently quite remote. Similarly, Japan's overseas peacekeeping operations have been low-key to the point of irrelevance. Japan's post-war arms procurement and arms build-up programs have given Japan's critics little cause for alarm. Therefore, Japan's neighbors have little to fear from a Japanese military build-up.

All of this might change with the political resurrection of the maverick politician and military hawk, Ichiro Ozawa. Ozawa believes that peacekeeping operations (PKO) should allow Japanese troops to participate in direct combat operations. The situation in East Timor exemplifies Japan's inability to pack a punch. Special operations forces arrived from all over the world to enforce a peace in Japan's backyard. Every contributing nation sent their ninjas, their elite forces. Every country, that is, except Japan. They sent a handful of truck drivers and cooks. Their contribution even in their own backyard is derisory.

Japan's overseas PKOs to date have been choked with red tape—East Timor is only the latest in a long, sad litany. They have needed Japanese parliamentary approval and the absolute acquiescence of every country involved in the specific PKO. Ozawa wants to change this. Ozawa wants Japan's peacekeeping forces to take on the same pro-active role all other countries do. Ozawa would like to see PKO and its extensions—disaster relief and humanitarian operations—become a major operational and force-building rationale.

Although this would seem a fairly non-contentious goal, Japan's very limited peacekeeping experiences to date do not augur well for the future. A brief review shows why. When the 1994 Rwandan genocide crisis erupted, the United States appealed to its Japanese ally for help. Japan sent a military medical and transport contingent to Goma, Zaire. However, the United States left them in the lurch. The United States forces went home the week before the Japanese arrived, effectively destroying the Japan Self-Defense Forces's (JSDF) attempts to contribute to the relief effort. The United States didn't even provide the strategic airlift they promised. The Japanese troops arrived in Goma on chartered Russian aircraft, and, deprived of the key logistical back-up their American allies had promised, they were utterly useless. The mission was a disaster.

Nor was Zaire an isolated case. When Japan rushed aid to Honduras following the devastation of Hurricane Mitch, American help was not forthcoming. Unable to operate so far from home without the logistical back up the Americans had promised, the Japanese contingent had to scurry home to Japan after just two weeks, even though hundreds of Hondurans were showing up daily seeking their assistance. These typical examples underline the problems a more forthright Japanese defense policy entails. When push comes to shove, Japan cannot depend on her main ally, the United States. This does not augur well for Japan's long-term defense.

Japan's long years of military dependence on the United States dulled her reflexes and blinkered her strategic vision. Tokyo has adopted not so much a hedgehog defense as an ostrich-like defense. Keeping its head firmly ensconced in the mercurial sands of economic development and the American military umbrella, it has ignored the evolving threats China and Asia's other emerging tiger economies pose to her vital interests. Japan's $250 million commitment to research into the Theater Missile Defense (TMD) program shows a much more realistic position. The TMD umbrella would cover not just Japan, Korea, and Taiwan but encroach into parts of Mainland China as well. The ubiquitous checkbook aside, it would mean Japan developing a closer military liaison with her key neighbors, South Korea and Taiwan in particular.

This would necessarily complicate her position vis-à-vis China. Since 1949, Japan's relationship with China has been an unstable and fundamentally precarious one. The pain of Japan's former policies still festers. China believes Japan's deliberately ambiguous 1997 declaration to be active in the event of unrest in areas adjacent to Japan is aimed at containing China—and she is accordingly wary of all Japan's overtures, both military and civilian. Because Japan now has the world's third largest military budget, Japanese remilitarization under the Mutual Security Treaty makes a variety of scenarios possible—scenarios that can frustrate China or complement her designs.

China's regional strategy has already been covered in previous chapters. She believes she should still be the dominant Middle Kingdom of old and that her neighbors should not try to overturn that particular apple cart. Although Tibet and other areas she has long since annexed have little choice in all of this, Japan does. In particular, China can either strengthen or loosen her ties with the United States.

China sees the U.S.-Japan alliance as its nemesis. This alliance, which has underwritten regional security since 1945, has frustrated China's national ambitions for almost as long. Currently, the Japanese navy works very closely with its American counterpart in fulfilling their regional duties. The two navies share information, technology, equipment, supplies, and resources; they work, operate, and train together; and, to a large degree, they trust, respect, and depend on each other at all operational levels. Even though the American Seventh Fleet dominates the relationship, the Japan Maritime Self-Defense Force (JMSDF) packs a solid punch itself. It operates, for example, 100 P3C anti-submarine aircraft, four times more than the number the United States maintains in the Seventh Fleet. Only Japan's constitution and the Seventh Fleet prevent it from realizing its full potential—and hinder China from pursuing her manifest destiny.

Although the U.S.-Japanese alliance appears rock-solid at present, it will be undermined by either continued economic rivalry between Japan and the United States or mounting U.S.-Chinese tensions that threaten Japanese involvement in a war with China. The first scenario is increasingly unlikely. China is now enjoying huge trade surpluses with the United States and has replaced Japan as the bugbear in public discourse of America's trade balance. As regards the latter scenario, should trade and other conflicts between China and the United States escalate, Japan could restructure the balance of power by pursuing an independent path or allying itself with China in pursuit of its economic interests. In theory, Japan would have to choose. In practice, Japan could not choose for one simple reason. The cornerstone of Japan's foreign policy is to ensure that the United States never becomes its adversary. Therefore, if Sino-American relations were to become frosty, Japan would have to side with the United States. China would have to take that into account.

Japan should not neglect Asia's large and potentially crucial markets. Far from it! Japan must pick the surest path that guarantees sustained economic growth in the coming years. Old markets must be solidified and newer ones won by caution and by degrees. Although Japan has had long-running clashes over economic policy with the United States, her clashes with the emerging Asian powers will be more brutal in the years to come. For those economies to achieve the levels of prosperity Japan enjoys, they will have to gnaw into Japan's traditional markets. All of that will lead to intra-Asian friction, which will be so much fuel on an already smoldering fire. Japan will have to choose sides in the disputes that follow.

Japan is faced with the dilemma of protecting her interests in Asia while not unduly unsettling any of the emerging powers there. Japan has to ensure that her imports and exports are not impeded.

Specifically, she must ensure that her food and oil imports are not threatened in the event of a major trade dispute erupting. For this, she needs a strong navy, which can command an inexorable technical lead over potential regional enemies. By far, the biggest potential enemy is the PRC. Japan must keep her technical lead over this giant Colossus, which skulks nearby. Because the demographic imperative lies so overwhelmingly with China, Japan must depend on technology and on more military alliances.

Japan must be an Asian equivalent of a Switzerland with the important caveat that the American alliance should be preserved and further ones with Australia, South Korea and her other neighbors should be built. Japan must have an army like Switzerland's, sufficiently strong to deter aggression but not strong enough to encourage aggression.

Although Japan is at least 15 years away from having a credible blue water navy, she already possesses formidable maritime teeth. The Japanese navy operates to over 1,000 miles from Japanese shores. She has the most modern and substantial navy in the Far East. Japan's navy exists to defend Japan's vital interests. Among the most vital of these are the sea-lanes through which Japan imports $30 bn of oil a year. The most important of these sea-lanes skirt the Spratly Islands and the very narrow Straits of Malacca through which much of this oil flows. China, through its toehold in Myanmar, could close off these sea-lanes in the future. One only has to look at their Taiwanese blockade to see the validity of this hypothesis. Japan's long-term naval strategy entails being ready, willing and able to protect these sea-lanes in the face of a determined but limited attack from China or an imploding Indonesia on them.

Although Japan has a formidable navy, she has not bared her claws in over fifty years. To coin Chairman Mao's immortal phrase, the Japanese navy is a paper tiger. There will have to be a significant change in Japanese public opinion before this situation corrects itself. Although the Japanese navy may have lost its stomach, the Chinese navy certainly hasn't. They have the fire in their belly and they have their objectives of securing the Spratlys and Taiwan to keep them focused.

Japan, meanwhile, procrastinates to a degree that would have driven Hamlet himself into a frenzy. And, as Japan procrastinates, China and North Korea are finessing their offensive missile technology. Militarily, the best way to stop the offensive missiles of North Korea and China is to destroy them on the offensive nation's home turf, either in the early stages of flight or on the ground. However, Japan's constitution forbids such offensive actions. Japan must instead concentrate on TMD. And, if TMD ever eventuates, Japan will have to give more than her customary signed check. She might have to give blood as well—whether she wants to or not.

North Korea's Taepodong-1 missile has most of Japan within its range. However, because the Taepodong-1 does not have the pinpoint accuracy needed to hit military targets, Japan still has the potential to develop viable counter strategies. Because almost all of Japan is within fifteen minutes of most North Korean and Chinese missiles, the coordination of space, sensor, aerodynamics, and communication technologies is vital to Japan's defense. The building blocks for such a defensive set up include: satellite remote-sensing capability to monitor possible launch preparations and pinpoint the infra-red flare of a launch; radar systems; and defensive-missile systems to intercept and destroy the incoming warhead. The best way of doing this is to destroy the incoming missile outside the atmosphere or to render it harmless through disintegration in the upper atmosphere. This will be no easy job. The cost will be gigantic—$50 billion or more at a minimum. Taiwan, which has substantial missile defense capabilities of its own, and South Korea, which faces imminent destruction should Pyongyang ever fulfill its promise of turning it into a sea of fire, would have to join in the mutual defense pact to make it cost effective. The forest of technology involved would be too advanced and far ranging for Japan to master on its own. Japan, which has developed certain trees of knowledge, could not develop and bring to fruition the required forest all on its own. This would be all the more so in the face of a belligerent China or a resurgent Russia. Thus, Japan must make choices.

This is all the more so as America's long process of disengagement from Asia continues. America, still licking its wounds from Vietnam, will not get sucked into another major conflict on the Asian mainland as long as the status quo holds. As long as she is confident Japan, her pivotal Asian domino, will not fall, America will let sleeping dogs lie. America's post-war Asian strategy was to make Japan a rich island fortress to prevent the Soviet Union and China further eroding the American position in Asia. America's Asian policy allowed Japan to grow economically, as long as its military remained emasculated and the American policy of preventing Japan from falling into the hands of hostile forces allied to China and the Soviet Union was maintained. Japan was allowed to fill the number two slot as long as it recognized America's right to the number one spot. That consolation prize has worked well for Japan.

The San Francisco Treaty, which effectively ended the Pacific War, was crafted in a manner to allow the United States to dominate both the Pacific and East Asia. A series of postwar bilateral treaties tied each of America's Asian allies separately to the United States and minimized autonomous collaboration between them. The system was modeled as a bicycle wheel with the United States as the hub and the individual Asian countries as spokes, each autonomously soldered by individual alliances with the United States. This spokes-and-hub structure maximized the dependence of Japan, Korea, South Vietnam, Taiwan and the other countries on the United States and thereby established the structure for the longterm U.S. hegemony in the Asia-Pacific region that followed.

Japan remained only one small chess piece in the world game America was playing with the Soviet Union, America's main adversary from 1945 to 1989. The advent of the Cold War did not alter the place of either Asia or Japan in American global priorities. Even during the Korean War, Europe remained the main theater for the United States. Simply put, East Asia ranked third behind Europe and the Mediterranean as areas of concern for America's military planners. The American Joint Chiefs of Staff (JCS) were well satisfied with a treaty that denied Japan's resources to their Soviet and Chinese enemies and provided bases that blocked the regional expansionist plans of the PRC and the Soviet Union. The war, if it came, would be fought and won elsewhere.

Fundamental to the entire system was the Mutual Security Treaty, forced on Japan as the price for ending the formal U.S. military occupation. The Mutual Security Treaty legitimized the presence of U.S. bases in Japan. These bases served multiple functions: encirclement of the Soviet Union (and now Russia) and China; training and jumping off points for U.S. foreign military intervention; command and intelligence sources for U.S. forces; and a lever to influence Japanese politics and contain Japanese military ambitions. Fifty-nine thousand U.S. troops are still based or home-ported at more than one hundred Japanese installations. Japan, in other words, stays firmly in America's camp.

Although Japan remained important to the JCS in the 1950s, the emphasis was on denying control of Japan's main islands to the enemy. In the event of war with the Soviet Union, American plans called for the withdrawal of troops from South Korea and the establishment of defensive positions on Japan's offshore island chain. Tactical air power would defend the approaches to these islands and the navy would also have shifted primarily to a defensive posture. The bases in Japan provided essential logistical support for America's other Asian allies and housed the Seventh Fleet's massive oil reserves. Faced with the wide-scale protests of the 1960s, the United States JCS decided that they should maintain their bases in Japan but lower their profile on the home islands by cutting further their ground forces stationed there. Okinawa would be the linchpin of linchpins.

The most serious challenge to the U.S.-Japan security treaty since the end of the Cold War came from the 1995 rape by three U.S. Marines stationed in Okinawa of a young Japanese schoolgirl. When the U.S. military refused to surrender the rapists to the local authorities, huge protests rocked the island. The Governor of Okinawa, Masahide Ota, refused to sign an administrative order forcing landowners to release their real estate for continued use by the U.S. forces. The governor argued that if Tokyo believed the Japan-US security treaty so essential to the nation's security, then most of the occupation forces should be transferred to the main islands. Although the protests have since died out, hard-core resentment remains. The locals see little benefit in being protected by an army of rapists.

The 1995 gang rape was only one in a series which began in the closing months of World War II, when American troops raped thousands of local women when they finally overran the island. The attacks continue to this day. In July 2000, another marine was apprehended trying to rape a 14-year-old in her family home. Although the local marine commander, Lieutenant General Earl B Hailston, visited the governor of Okinawa, Keiichi Inamine, and made a formal bow of contrition—the first such apology from a senior U.S. military, made even more remarkable for the fact that it was made before the marine had been formally charged—the locals have had enough. They want the rapists gone.

This local opposition has muddied the overall picture. Like the European alliances they were modeled on, America's Asian treaties were designed to keep Japan, the former enemy, down and the new communist powers out. They also provided assurances that the Americans would remain in control. But there is no European equivalent to the role the Korean and Chinese treaties played in restraining America's allies from embarking on their own campaigns against the enemy. The Asian system, if it can be called that, also lacked the locally inspired efforts at integrated defense planning that preceded the Atlantic alliance. Finally, and most significantly, Japan has yet to assume the role in Asia Germany plays in NATO. Therefore, unlike the European and NATO alliances, the Asian ones were fundamentally flawed. There was an inherent contradiction in them. America—the outsider—was central to the defense of Asia, a different continent far removed from it.

After South Vietnam, Cambodia, and Laos all fell to the communist insurgents, America and her remaining allies reassessed the whole matrix of their strategies and tactics. Some very important policies emerged as a result. The United States government announced that though it would maintain its treaty commitments in Asia, it would fight no more ground wars there. Deterrence became the objective of U.S. deployments rather than potential war fighting capability. This essentially means that, in the final analysis, it is Asian not American blood that will be spilled in any ground war on the Korean Peninsula or Taiwan. Logically, much of that blood will be Japanese.

Japan's American alliance is not therefore as omnipotent as it once was. This is particularly the case in the area's main flash points of the Korean peninsula and Taiwan. There is more than a distinct possibility that these countries will be either annexed by hostile powers or will be subsumed into their camp for reasons of self-survival. Japan cannot stand idly by and allow that to happen. She must make the requisite choices. Japan must prepare for when the Seventh Fleet sails home. She must find new allies.

The cornerstone of any Asian-centered defense alliance must be closer economic, diplomatic and military links between South Korea and Japan. The historical enmity, which has existed between these two powers, is a noxious thread that worms its way through this book—and a thousand others. Relations between Japan and South Korea were only normalized as recently as 1965 at the Treaty on Basic Relations. Among other things, Japan agreed to provide $800 million in economic assistance, which spurred the Korean economy and significantly reduced the economic burden on the United States of maintaining the Republic of Korea against North Korean aggression.

Reflecting Japan's traditional vulnerability, Tokyo actually went a bit further than writing Seoul this generous check. In 1969 President Nixon, as part of his Nixon Doctrine of placing greater responsibility on Asian nations for their own security, persuaded Japanese Prime Minister Eisaku Sato to state in a joint U.S.-Japan communiqué that the security of the Republic of Korea was essential to Japan's own security. The Korea clause, as this became known, was the foundation stone of Japan's contribution to regional security. It was also an essential element of the U.S. agreement to return Okinawa to Japan, because it guaranteed freedom of action by United States forces stationed in Okinawa and elsewhere in Japan in case of a military threat to South Korea.

So far, however, Japan's Korean bluff has not been called. North Korea has been playing a cat and mouse game with it and Japan so far has not risen to the bait. As things currently stand, there is little Japan can do, save producing its checkbook and pulling at America's apron strings to counter North Korea's missiles. Neither of these strategies impresses North Korea. Japan must change its stance if it wants to be taken seriously. Japan must develop the potential to autonomously counter North Korea's aggression.

Nuclear proliferation means that the stakes are getting higher all the time and the loose cannon of North Korea does not help the resolution of matters. Because East Asia is now a nuclear chessboard, the players must move with caution. Unlike the Cold War standoff, there is now a multiplicity of players to complicate matters. Although Japan is most definitely one of these players, the chance of a strategic miscalculation is immense when maverick countries like North Korea are allowed strut across the playing field.

Japan's nuclear forays are giving its ancient enemies cause to pull in their horns. Tokyo has stockpiled over 100 tons of plutonium that would be relatively simple to transform into weapons grade material. Japan's fast-breeder reactors (FBRs) have the capacity to squeeze over 60 times more energy from uranium fuel than can the light-water reactors of most other countries. Japan will, in other words, have the capacity to make more nuclear weapons than the combined arsenals of the United States and Russia hold. If nothing else, this arsenal makes an impressive bundle of bargaining chips.

Given the region's proliferation of nuclear warheads, Japan's massive stockpile is no bad thing. Pakistan and India have now both joined the nuclear club. India's program is as much designed to deter China, as it is to get Pakistan off its back. India's Agni II rocket has a range of 2,500 kilometers and this puts a large chunk of China within range. China has her own impressive arsenal and, though Chairman Mao dismissed nuclear weapons as a paper tiger, theirs is a tiger that packs a particularly lethal punch. Asia's major powers are increasingly going down the militaristic road and, if Japan wants her voice heard, she will have to have military teeth as well. This entails the acquisition of nuclear weapons, either through the American umbrella proxy or through autonomous development as India has done.

Their neutralization of China and Pakistan apart, India's armed forces are as major a destabilizing force in the region as are the certifiable leaders of North Korea. India's Prithvi ballistic missile, its Arjun tank and its entire Agni missile-technology program all raise the prospects of strategic miscalculation in the region. A nationalistic Indian government might engage in an arms race as a diversionary tactic. India's development of the bomb has not only raised the stakes with Pakistan but has boosted the BJP's domestic popularity as well. The BJP harnessed India's 1998 nuclear tests for its own nefarious reasons.

Because they might even use the bomb for their own populist reasons, India's xenophobic political leaders are more dangerous than India's vast army is. India's current posture would reserve nuclear weapons as an option of last resort, meant to deter Pakistan from using nuclear weapons first. The advantage of this approach is that it does not require elaborate and expensive specialized delivery and command-and-control systems. If nuclear war broke out between the two neighbors, the Indian Air Force's existing strike aircraft could deliver a retaliatory nuclear blow. The armed forces support this approach on cost grounds. It is affordable and does not threaten the funds they need to maintain their conventional forces, the key to winning a non-nuclear war with Pakistan. After all, if India's nuclear weapons successfully deter Pakistani first use of nuclear weapons, superior conventional forces would still be needed to fight and win the inevitable conventional war that would then follow.

The more likely scenario is that the nationalist BJP will support the nuclear development option and run the strategic miscalculation risks this involves. If Agni is tested, produced and deployed as a nuclear system, the prospects for the conventional modernization budget are that much worse, as are the hopes that India will stick with its Pakistan-oriented, last-resort nuclear posture. The only way to justify Agni when existing strike aircraft are so much better suited to the tasks of deterrence is to invent a provocative new justification for taking the missile route. China would unquestionably be the external threat justifying an Indian nuclear build-up—and the concomitant risk of strategic miscalculation. China, needless to say, would not be amused. She would escalate her own programs in retaliation. The results would be too dire to contemplate.

This is no idle speculation. Both World Wars I and II were started by smaller miscalculations. If the nuclear genie escapes in Asia, she will never be put back into the bottle. Nuclear war will result.

Japan must take this evolving situation into account. Times have changed since Japanese Prime Minister Sató Eisaku got the Nobel Prize in 1975 for stipulating that Tokyo would neither make nor deploy nuclear weapons, nor allow them to pass through Japanese territory. Because Japan now finds itself a target for North Korean missiles, she must develop not only treaties with India but also her own nuclear defense weapons as well as the means to deliver them. More than any other country in the world, Japan is uniquely placed to develop such weapons. She also has the power of delivery. She must then use this power to make the others sit down at the bargaining table. Without nuclear weapons, Japan is only a military mouse. The nuclear card will give the Japanese mouse her voice.

Because its major challenges will come from the air, Japan has developed formidable antiaircraft and antiballistic missile defense systems. Japan's radar and its accurate Tomahawk missile technology are improvements on their American prototypes. Japan's H-2 rockets are the best ICBMs in the world. Japan's civilian expertise in opto-electronics is very useful militarily in such state-of-the-art weaponry as smart bombs. More to the point, when they were tested in combat, they passed with flying colors. They allowed the United States to destroy Hanoi's Red River Bridge after America had conspicuously failed to demolish it after years of trying. They also proved very reliable in the USAF's more recent forays into Baghdad and Belgrade. Other Japanese strengths in miniaturization, automation, telecommunications and the development of durable, lightweight, advanced materials will further enhance their military capabilities.

Japan's plutonium purchases have allowed it to develop the nuclear submarine technology to counter China's blue water navy. Though impressive, a handful of nuclear submarines and a couple of batteries of missile defenses do not make Japan impregnable. There are countervailing forces at work.

Bizarre as it seems, Japan's expertise in these niche areas is a cause for concern in Washington. America fears losing market share if Japan begins to export its expertise—and, to develop the required expertise, Japan would have to copy the examples of Sweden, South Africa and other small countries and aggressively export. The United States fears that this would be at its expense. Japan's rising capabilities in dual-use technologies have intensified these concerns. Japanese technological capabilities in commercial fields related to military use threatens the preeminent position American producers currently enjoy in the world's arms markets. This is ironic as, historically, the United States encouraged Japan in its development of dual use capabilities. Spin-offs from the radio industry, for example, helped kick-start the Japanese commercial television industry, which eventually obliterated their American competitors. As recently as the 1980s, Japan benefited more than any other American ally from licensed production. The peak of licensing activity was reached in the late 1980s with the Patriot surface-to-air missile co-production program, which resulted in the licensing and transfer of virtually every element of hardware and early generations of software in the system. Although Japanese production of the Patriot missiles and launchers has come to a close, this program continues with various upgrade packages.

Others, however, followed. By far the most significant politically of these was the FSX/F-2 co-development program, which utilized the U.S. F-16 fighter aircraft as its prototype. Although the FSX program brought many issues to a head, the crucial question to be asked is this: should Japan have an independent deterrent policy or should the United States remain as its main military supplier? Although arms transfers are a proportionately minor part of trade between America and Japan, they do hit on some raw nerves.

These sore points have reemerged as Japan and the United States ponder how to pay for TMD. The idea of ballistic-missile defenses re-emerged in Washington after North Korea's 1993 missile test, but really assumed their present importance when Pyongyang lobbed its three-stage rocket across northern Japan in 1998. This test alarmed Washington. U.S. military intelligence analysts concluded that Pyongyang could hit American troops and allies across the whole East Asian theater. The entire western United States seaboard is now within range of North Korea's nuclear and chemical warheads. After the first North Korean missile splashed down in the Sea of Japan in 1993, Tokyo and Washington began urgent negotiations on ways to come up with a working missile defense for the archipelago. They concluded that TMD had to get priority but disagreed on how to fund it. Washington wants Japan to buy U.S. technology virtually off the shelf and help finance the new Star Wars scheme, something Tokyo is loath to do. The Japanese, for their part, want U.S. technological help to develop their own systems. Although this debate is pursued in the next chapter, the Japanese dilemma is plain. Because they are in the line of fire, they want to be able to develop the protective shield themselves. America, for its own geostrategic reasons, does not want to see its allies develop this autonomy. Cost grounds alone would mean that they would all have to work together. The question then would be who would control the key technology. Because America does not want to be beholden to anyone else, she wants to retain the key technology under her own control. Although that is understandable from an American viewpoint, it is cold comfort to the Japanese.

Although the hunt to develop super-accurate hit-to-kill missiles is still in its infancy, the costs of developing even a prototype are gigantic. Much of the $10 billion in new development funds will go for theater missile defenses, including high-altitude interceptors, low-altitude interceptors and sea-based interceptors. The high-altitude devices have failed all five tests to which they have been submitted, the low-altitude ones have similarly failed four tests and the sea-based interceptors have never been tested at all. This makes the American security umbrella look increasingly leaky.

Current U.S. technologies are inadequate even to meet current missile threats. The Patriot's lack of success in defeating Iraq's primitive Scud missiles suggests that serious questions must be raised about the likely effectiveness of even Patriot upgrades. The fact that the U.S. military has opted for an alternative missile, the ERINT, for its own follow-on system, the PAC-3, indicates that currently deployed Patriot systems may have been over-sold to Taiwan and other U.S. allies in East Asia. This has done nothing to assuage Japan's opposition to America's plans to control the TMD technology—and, consequently, the defenses of Japan as well. In fairness, there are certain short-range missiles that some of these systems might stop effectively, especially a relatively small number of missiles launched in an individual sequence over time. However, barrage attacks or the use of decoys, sub-munitions, and counter-measures would likely overwhelm them. China will eventually have this capability in the theaters adjacent to Japan.

Pyongyang is already deploying them. There are simply too many North Korean missiles that can reach Seoul in too short a period of time for present defense systems to be effective. Seoul, in other words, can be turned into a sea of fire any time Pyong-yang chooses to light the match. The only ultimate solution to Asia's missile proliferation problems, therefore, must combine military and political solutions. Japan must take the lead in pro-moting both TMD and the more long-term political policies that will make Beijing less likely to use missiles in the first place. Part of this must entail the unification of Korea and the dismantling of the Pyongyang regime. Theirs is one dagger that must be per-manently decommissioned. In the meantime, the defense plan-ners of South Korea and Japan must decide how best to neutralize Pyongyang's threat. In this connection, former United States Sec-retary of Defense William Cohen issued a stern warning to South Korea against purchasing Russia's cheaper S-300V TMD system. Although this has put visible strains in the relations between Washington and Seoul over TMD, it does not really distract from the main objective of securing an integrated, overall policy response from Japan and her allies.

Japan must reinforce the American alliance while at the same time building up its economic relations with the Russian Far East. Japan must use its checkbook to eliminate the Russian threat and TMD while keeping China on side at the same time. This is cer-tainly what Taiwan wants. Taiwan has been a more fervent sup-porter of near-term TMD than either South Korea or Japan. The PRC's missile launchers parked nearby have seen to that. Notably, it is alone among these erstwhile allies in deploying its own TMD weapons—the Tien Kung series. Its newest system, the Tien Kung-3, has the capability to destroy ballistic missiles as well as cruise missiles, giving it an advantage over expected TMD capabilities. It might also provide an exit strategy for the United States: continuing its naval support role, but lowering its TMD profile and developing instead a more balanced diplomatic position to enable it to abandon Taiwan without undue domestic repercussions. Japan, in assessing this further risk of abandonment, would have to take the dynamics of American domestic politics into account. Again, Japan would have to choose between continuing to skulk under America's security umbrella and developing an alternative, more proactive strategy to employ when Uncle Sam removes his brolly.

The ultimate criteria for TMD deployments in East Asia must be whether they increase or decrease regional security and tension, whether they serve to foment rivalries and make war more likely, or whether they lead the region to peace. Although belligerents always have to talk in the end, it is better to talk—or to avoid battle at all—from a position of strength. The next chapter assesses Japan's capabilities to do just that.

Chapter
SIX

Japan's Military Machine

Japan's defense industry is an inconsequential part of Japan's overall industrial sector and strategy. It accounts for less than one percent of Japanese GDP and even those firms that are most heavily involved in the sector depend on it for only a modest part of their sales and profits. Firms, like Mitsubishi Heavy Industries (MHI) and Kawasaki Heavy Industries (KHI), have traditionally involved themselves in the sector because of the spin-off technological benefits it has given them. The brakes of the bullet train, for example, were based on the brakes for the F-104 Starfighter, which MHI built under license in the 1960s. The F-104 also gave MHI the expertise to develop the T-2, Japan's first indigenous jet aircraft. These almost incidental benefits aside, the Japanese defense industry has yielded few gains to Japan.

Japan's defense industry differs markedly from most other industrialized Western countries, where arms manufacturers rely primarily on defense contracts to stay afloat. Japan's defense industry is dominated by large, over-diversified companies like Mitsubishi and Kawasaki that engage in weapons production almost as an aside—almost as a hobby—in the hope that knowledge gained will have applications elsewhere in their core activities. Under no circumstances can the Japanese defense industry be considered crucial to any of Japan's major companies. Although the top five Japanese defense contractors win over 60 percent of the contracts awarded by the JDA, the military side of their business generates no more than one-fifth of their total revenues and much less than that for most of the firms engaged in the industry. They are not crucial to them. Instead, these firms depend on spin-off benefits in their civilian enterprises to recoup their investments. In this, they differ markedly from the United States, where tough procurement regulations force America's defense contractors to build strong barriers between their civilian and military sectors. Their different histories have shaped the differing objectives of Japanese and American defense firms.

America's defense industry was geared to serve America's superpower role. America's military research and development efforts were predicated on winning significant technological breakthroughs to develop the necessary advanced weapons systems victory in the Cold War demanded. Because Japan's approach was geared as much to finding commercial applications as anything else, it has become particularly attractive to the United States in the post-Cold War world, where trade wars have now assumed higher priorities. Further, as the MHI case outlined above exemplifies, defense procurement allows Japanese industries to achieve cutting-edge knowledge that they can apply to commercial advantage elsewhere. Many of the arguments for *kokusanka*, for the indigenization of the defense industry, hinge on being able to exploit synergies between the civilian and military sectors. However, although developing the required expertise is essential, this becomes redundant if production and sales are not allowed. These are needed to recoup the research and development costs. These costs cannot be recouped under license agreements—unless dual uses manifest themselves. Formerly, as in the case with MHI and the bullet train, Japanese companies could recoup their investments by finding commercial uses in the non-military sector for the expertise they developed in the military sector. This is becoming an increasingly unlikely scenario as Washington progessively prices these spin-off applications into their licensing arrangements. Washington's more niggardly attitude is not the only new complication. The growing importance of the electronics sector in defense has changed this scenario somewhat. These latter firms have almost exclusively civilian contracts and are, by and large, not very interested in the defense sector at all. These firms, if pushed to decide, would be as happy to leave the sector altogether as to stay in it.

This presents a dilemma to Japanese strategic planners. The firms they most heavily depend on to keep their competitive edge in the defense industry are not particularly attracted to it. Because defense is peripheral to their main commercial activities, they feel little if any historical or pecuniary loyalty to it. This was not always the case. Japan's large defense firms had been at the center of Japanese economic life from the time of the 1894–95 war with China to the surrender of August 1945. The need for military self-sufficiency gave rise to the Japanese *zaibatsu* at the end of the nineteenth century. The "Enrich the country, strengthen the military" slogan needed a well-equipped army. The *zaibatsus* were the ticket to achieve this—and the militarization that followed. Because the *zaibatsus* played such a key role in Imperial Japan, McArthur dismantled them. He also banned the research, development, and production of weapons, battleships, and aircraft. This effectively put the Japanese defense industry into cold storage, if not ultimately terminal decline. *Kokusanka* has been an intermittent effort to reverse this trend.

Proponents of *kokusanka* and of rearmament were faced with almost insuperable odds: Japanese public opinion, McArthur, the Ministry of Finance's budgetary objections, and the Yoshida doctrine, which preached economic revival with minimal remilitarization. From the first internal fight over licensed production of the F-86 saber jet in the early 1950s through the critical FSX debacle of the 1980s and today's arguments over TMD, the same arguments have raged around Japan's need to achieve technological and military autonomy, while at the same time developing her industrial might and not endangering the American alliance. Although the debate has been long and intensive, little of real substance has changed. Although Japan has developed large pockets of defense-related expertise, she is still heavily dependent on the United States for most of her defense needs. Because of this, Japan continues to run the risks of either entrapment or abandonment. Because of Japan's failure to develop an effective and autonomous deterrent, Japan continues to run the risk that America may either drag her into a war she does not want or it may abandon Japan for another Asian power, China being the most obvious example. *Kokusanka*, the argument goes, would give Japan insurance against such scenarios.

Kokusanka, the indigenization of defense procurement, has been a recurrent theme in Japan since the Occupation ended. Subsequent attempts at *kokusanka*, at achieving some form of self-sufficiency in the defense industry, had to overcome not only the objections of Japan's American allies but a deep-seated public aversion to the downside of a militarist revival—Japan, lest we forget, is the only country that has been at the receiving end of nuclear weapons. Although that latter concern is dealt with later, this chapter's main focus is on Japan's prospects for *kokusanka*, and the consequences this implies for the American alliance. First of all though, it examines how the defense sector fits into Japan's overall economic setting. Because the two sectors have been integrated into Japan's overall industrial policy and because America has increasingly put Japan's dual uses of technology at the center of trade and defense discussions, Japan's modern defense industry can only be examined in the overall context of Japan's total industrial complex.

Although Japan's military needs once dominated Japan's economic policy to the exclusion of most other sectors, now the military sector is inconsequential and Japan Inc. is synonymous with failed banks and over-capacity in the auto and electronic industries. *Japan's Big Bang*, published by Tuttle's in 2000, outlined how Tokyo's policies led to the Japanese crash, which was, in monetary terms, the biggest financial crash in world history. The book showed that Japan's banks are all technically bankrupt and that even solvent Japanese companies are finding the going tough. The book recorded the lack of a legal and accounting infrastructure, which are necessary to maintain a modern economy. It stated that wide-scale restructuring was needed to revive Japan's competitiveness. Nowhere, as we shall see, is that more apparent than in the defense sector. Before we discuss that sector, it is best to make a slight detour into the auto and electronics industries, which are both at the heart of the entire Japanese industrial empire—and at the fringes of Japan's defense industry as well.

The Land of the Rising Sun is also the Land of the Vanishing Car Companies. Japanese car companies can produce about 12 million cars a year. Currently, less than 5 million cars are being sold each year in Japan. Japan has 554 cars per 1,000 people, lower than America's 791 per 1,000. Japan's car ownership ratio, however, is much higher than Europe's, even though Japan has fewer roads and parking spaces than Europe. Indeed, so precious are Tokyo parking spaces that prospective car buyers must produce documentation that they own a car park before the police will allow their purchase to be effected. Auto companies, eager to solve their own problems by selling more cars on the protected and congested domestic market, dominate Japanese television commercials.

So far, the massive restructuring, which has occurred in the global auto markets, has yet to impinge itself on Japan. Whereas the much bigger United States market has three local carmakers, Japan, with only 40 percent of the population of the United States, has eleven car and truck makers. The Japanese eleven span the range from companies such as Toyota and Honda that are, by any yardstick, internationally competitive to those that are, even by Japan's own elastic standards, grossly inefficient. Though Japan's recession has put the squeeze on all eleven, Nissan and Mitsubishi, both of which have substantial military contracts, are particularly hurting. With Toyota retaining its vice-like grip on 40 percent of the domestic market, the end result is massive over-capacity and an urgent need for massive rationalization. Mitsubishi and Nissan, despite Renault buying it, are the prime candidates for culling. They have lost whatever competitive edge they ever had.

This is of major importance to the defense industry. Nissan is a major supplier of military vehicles and the Mitsubishi group produce everything from ships, nuclear power stations and aircraft to missiles and tanks—and small run-around cars that lose money. Like so many other things in industrial Japan, this defies normal Western standards of logic. Although there may have been some slight synergies in having such a diverse industrial base in the past, greater specialization is needed to survive in today's more competitive—and specialized—environment. That explains why Volvo, the famous Swedish manufacturer, sold off its profitable car-making ventures. Because it wanted to concentrate on the more lucrative truck and bus sector, it took over Scania in August 1999 to become the world's second-largest truck and bus producer. Although this makes eminent sense in Sweden—which has, incidentally, a thriving defense sector—it makes little sense to the Japanese. Kawasaki, after all, makes motorbikes—and battleships.

Although Nissan has sold out to Renault, Mitsubishi is still hanging in. Quite simply, a firm such as Mitsubishi that builds nuclear power stations, battleships and fighter aircraft should not be dabbling around in the glutted small car market. The competition is too stiff and there are no worthwhile synergies with their larger, defense related projects. One or the other must go. They must specialize.

Mitsubishi is part of a wider agglomeration of industrial and financial companies of particular concern to us here. They are a primary defense contractor, making everything from battleships to run-around cars. The Japanese call these alliances *keiretsus* and the weird *keiretsu* that can see synergies in producing battleships and small cars might well decide to keep Mitsubishi's motor division afloat for their own peculiar reasons. This is in total contrast to the West. When Rolls Royce, for example, took over Vickers in 1999, they were criticized for diversifying within the defense industry. Although there was some logic and some synergies in Rolls Royce acquiring Vickers' maritime engine technology, there is none at all in Mitsubishi making everything from paper napkins to nuclear power stations.

The damage for Mitsubishi does not end there. Mitsubishi Electric is losing vast sums of money in a large variety of their electronic industries. These span the audiovisual, information systems and semi-conductors sectors. Their core businesses include communications infrastructure such as fiber optic cables and satellite communications, high-quality image processing, Internet and Intranet security, mass communication systems, and wireless telephony. These are all fast-growing or highly profitable with important defense related applications. If Mitsubishi divested itself of its autos and other peripheral, loss-making ventures and concentrated on where it could add value, their prospects would be much brighter than they now are. This would entail a fundamental change on the part of this industrial giant—and of its competitors. Four out of Japan's five electrical conglomerates are floundering under the weight of collapsing domestic demand and repeated poundings from falling silicon chip prices. Whereas Hitachi, NEC, Mitsubishi Electric, and Toshiba are losing big money, Fujitsu is transforming itself from a company dependent on hardware production to one whose main source of growth is software and services. Like Japan's car companies and like Japan itself, the other four are stuck in the old and obsolete ways of the past.

This is not good news for Japan. Between them, these five

electronic firms account for more than 25 percent of Japan's exports. They employ over a million workers. And only Fujitsu is making profits! The markets for their key products are glutted. And, amazingly given their past versatility, they struggle to cope in today's globalized markets. As electronic product life cycles shorten, they cannot focus in on the areas that will give them sustainable advantage. These companies, whose semiconductors and superconductors sparked major trade wars with the United States in the 1980s, and whose telecommunications equipment, cooling systems and elevators set world standards in previous decades, have lost their way. They concentrated on hardware and glutted the markets they conquered. The U.S. competitors they conquered stepped deftly aside and claimed the new and more lucrative software and services as their own.

In their rise to prominence, these companies developed strategies that have since become barriers to further progress. Japan Inc. spent over $500 million annually lobbying Capitol Hill. Toshiba Electric spent a great deal of this on a battery of lawyers, lobbyists and public relations men, who all proved useful when they were caught selling computer-controlled milling machines to the Soviet navy. Because this mercenary act enabled the Soviet Union's nuclear submarines to evade U.S. radar, Toshiba were almost locked out of the entire U.S. market altogether. So too were other companies. Toshiba's act brought a range of other American defense-related complaints to the fore. These included Tokyo's patent process and allegations of wholesale spying by MITI.

American companies felt with considerable justification that Tokyo's patent registration processes were as much a spy and copy exercise as they were attempts to honestly assess competing American technologies. Japanese companies got nylon from Du Pont, color televisions from RCA, transistors from Bell Laboratories and the VCR from Ampex. They made all of these their own. All in all, Japan has bought and licensed a whole range of technologies and has made over $1 trillion by conservative estimates.

Although many of these dubiously conducted technological transfers served America's defense needs of revitalizing Japan, times have now changed. Japan is able to compete head-to-head with the United States on a wide variety of industrial fronts. Defense, however, is one of the few areas where the advantage continues to rely with the United States. This advantage is not as absolute as it once was. Whereas America still retains the forest of knowledge necessary to be a world power, Japan has acquired several formidable trees of knowledge of its own. Japan, in other words, has some fabulous defense-related engineering talents of its own. Hitachi and Sony, for example, lead the world in pinhead surveillance cameras. All six major digital camcorder makers are Japanese. The Japanese buy over 90 percent of the world's digital camcorders—1.5 million or thereabouts a year. Although this does little for Japan's export industry, it does quite a lot to develop her expertise in this vital area.

Often, this expertise spills over into the defense sector. Despite its Peace Constitution, Japan designs and produces a seemingly impressive array of high technology missiles, tanks, warships, and aircraft. MHI's Type-90 tank has the most sophisticated automation of any of today's modern tanks. KHI's T-4 jet trainer is the epitome of design efficiency. Toshiba and Mitsubishi Electric have created a portable surface-to-air missile that is far superior to the U.S. Stinger. There are countless more examples of where Japanese expertise in particular branches of defense knowledge easily outstrip their American equivalents. Some of the more important of these include the ducted rocket engine technology, a supersonic rocket engine technology superior to most competing technologies; millimeter-wave/infrared dual-mode seekers, missile-seeker technologies that enable better target detection and signal processing; closed-loop degaussing for steel hull ships, a technology that automatically monitors and reduces the magnetic signature of a steel hull ship and therefore makes them less vulnerable to attack; advanced steel for ships and armored vehicles, which reinforces the steel in naval vessel structures and combat vehicle armor; and fighting vehicle propulsion technology using ceramic material, a technology for low heat-rejection diesel engines in which ceramic coating and ceramic components are used on tanks and armored vehicles.

These important breakthroughs notwithstanding, the harsh reality remains that whereas Japan has some particularly strong trees of knowledge, the forest overwhelmingly belongs to America. Japan just does not have the logistical depth of America or the EU to be a major league player. While Japanese industry has established a global position in a wide range of critical modern technologies, Japan's defense industry has lagged behind. At the systems level, military technology has simply moved faster than Japan's ability to catch up. Japan, in other words, does not have an autonomous arms industry. Today, the defense industry accounts for less than 0.6 percent of total industrial production, an almost insignificant amount in Japan's overall context. Japan produces about 90 percent of its own military requirements. Much of that is built under license from U.S. firms and a considerable amount of the technology is black-boxed—sealed so that Japanese engineers cannot study and copy them.

Most of the big-ticket items in Japan's current defense plans continue to be imported directly from the U.S. assembly lines. These latter weapons include warning aircraft, Aegis vessels, F-15s and multiple launch rocket systems. In other words, although Japan has achieved significant breakthroughs in certain branches of knowledge, the choicest fruits of the forest remain firmly out of bounds for the present. The FSX debacle, which this chapter later discusses, merely highlights how complex are the interplay of technological and defense issues in this entire area. For the moment, it is important to return to Japan's world class industries to understand how largely irrelevant the country's defense needs are for it.

Opto-electronics, for example, is a vital component of smart bombs and other cutting edge military technologies. Canon's vast expertise in opto-electronics merely reflects the fact that blue-chip Japanese manufacturers are among the world's best. However, over 70 percent of Canon's sales and 30 percent of its production is outside Japan and, because of this, it is vulnerable to the adverse publicity defense contracts entail. Like all its competitors, it spends immense sums on research and development. Keen, cut-throat competition from Ricoh and Nikon keep it on its toes. It just does not have the time and energy to devote to the further problems a major realignment in the defense sector would give it.

Canon funds itself mostly on sales; its strong cash flows means it has little or no use for bank loans or defense related contracts that are not promptly paid. Founded in 1933, its first objective was to surpass Leica, the German precision camera maker. They have long since done that. Cameras, in fact, are now only 11 percent of sales whereas copiers, computer printers and fax machines form the bulk of its present sales. Canon controls much of the printer market and the expensive ink cartridges they run on. Given that Canon were slow to enter the digital era, they might end up struggling if the paperless office ever becomes a reality. They must devote their energies to staying abreast of developments in their rapidly core areas of activity. They don't need the hassles of defense contracts.

Though strong, they do not have much room for error. Canon's 11 percent return on equity, though high for Japan, is low by Western standards. Canon has never sacked workers to any significant degree and so has never had to contend with strikes. Because it continues to operate in diverse areas, where it enjoys no particular strategic advantage, this happy state of affairs cannot continue forever. It is just too exposed to its strong competitors to entertain dubious forays into the defense sector. The same goes for Sony. Sony, with $56 billion of annual sales and a 170,000 strong worldwide workforce, is a veritable Titan among Titans. However, Sony has troubles of its own. Its core electronics business is in trouble. Though accounting for 60 percent of sales, it yields less than 20 percent of its overall profits. Its strategic advantage does not lie there any more. This is because Sony is a high-cost producer with a world famous brand name. It relies on being nimble—on getting innovative gadgets to the market ahead of its rivals and charging a hefty premium of 30 percent or more on them. Because of this, defense contracts cannot figure prominently in their corporate strategy.

More generally still, Japanese companies enjoy too much protection and fail to properly modernize as a result. Nippon Telegraph and Telephone, for example, remains a monopoly in all but name. The Japanese government still owns 59 percent of the company and turns a blind eye to its anti-competitive practices. People and businesses still pay through the nose to own and operate phones in Japan. NTT still continues to dominate local calls, long distance calls, leased lines, cellular and data communications. Faced with increased competition from major world players such as Cable & Wireless and British Telecom, NTT has responded by exploiting its near monopoly on the home market even more. Like so much of corporate Japan, it is failing to bite the bullet and institute wide scale reform and rationalization.

Nor can Japan's leaders put too much emphasis on the defense sector. Japan's core industrial areas are under too much pressure from the forces of globalization to allow for such frivolities. Industrially, Japan has too much to lose and too little to gain to risk it all for what is now an inconsequential part of its overall portfolio.

The Japanese defense industry must be looked at as a smaller sub set of this bigger family of Japan Inc. for two reasons. The Japanese defense industry is a very small part of this overall whole and the Japanese defense industry depends on commercial applications to a much larger degree than any Western power. Although no modern state is fully autonomous in producing weapons of war, America, Russia, and China, the three countries of immediate concern to Japan, are as near to it as counts. Smaller states with substantial arms industries such as Sweden, Israel, and South

Africa depend on exports to defray their development costs. The special case of North Korea has already been dealt with at some length. Japan, debarred from exporting its products, depends on commercial spin-offs to stay at the forefront of the industry.

This is ultimately unsustainable. The Japanese government will continue to cut back on overall defense spending and it will continue to get big-ticket items from the United States. Because it will not be beefing up its defense spending or allowing Japan's defense contractors to export their weaponry, the overall prognosis for Japan's defense sector must be bad. Further, Japan's sluggish economy means that her defense contractors are less able to divert surplus workers in the defense sector to the civilian sector; the demand is just not there. The fact that Japan continues to buy AWACs (airborne warning and control systems), multiple-launch rocket systems and Aegis destroyers from America means that there is little left over to share among Japan's own defense companies. The AWACs, for example, cost about $500 million apiece and, when taken with all the other expensive items that Japan procures from its American ally, leaves little left over for the Japanese companies.

The sheer number of competing Japanese firms merely worsens this prognosis. Just as in the car industry, Japan has too many aerospace manufacturers. These include MHI, KHI, Fuji Heavy Industries (FHI), Ishikawajima-Harima Heavy Industries (IHI), ShinMaywa Industries, and Japan Aircraft Manufacturing Co. Competition among these domestic manufacturers is minimal—unlike the commercial automobile and electronics industries, where competition is intense among the firms involved in the sector. MHI dominates the jet aircraft industry and KHI and FHI are usually the main sub contractors. IHI usually produces the jet engines. These companies generally do not make any real money out of their defense contracts. They are there to learn skills that can be transferred to their civilian enterprises. They all need commercial spin-offs to make their military investments pay off. They are there for the more intangible benefits of experimenting with the spin-on applications of defense-related technology, developing systems integration experience and generally creating their own momentum in technology development.

Thus, while their strategies allow them to make some breakthroughs in specific areas, they cannot make the generational breakthroughs that the American stealth fighter typifies. This is because when American companies already know that they will be designing and manufacturing the successor to a system already under production, it allows them to take the necessarily long view on systems development and capital investment. They gain the freedom to invest in technologies or manufacturing capacity that may not yield truly economic results for a generation. Japanese *kokusanka* companies, by contrast, must make shorter-term profits indirectly through commercial spin-offs. Their road to profits is therefore less direct and usually less likely to succeed in either the commercial or military fields. Often, as in the case of MHI's short take-off jet, it fails at immense cost to both.

The Japanese defense industry is as distorted and glutted as any of Japan's more export oriented sectors. MHI continues to dominate with 25 percent of the market and KHI and IHI have about 19 percent of the market each. Mitsubishi Electronic Corporation (MELCO), Toshiba, NEC, FHI, Hitachi, Oki Electric, Fujitsu, and Nissan Motors are some of the other well-known companies supplying the industry. But within this tight family, there is grave overlap that surpasses even the commercial auto and electronics industries.

MHI, KHI, Ishikawajima, and Hitachi Zosen Corporation all compete with each other as well as with their foreign competitors to supply Japan's battleships, cruisers, and submarines. The military vehicle market is almost as congested, with MHI, Komatsu, Hitachi, and Nissan being the major suppliers. Japan's military aircraft suppliers include MHI, KHI, FHI, and Nissan. The military electronics industry has a veritable army of companies supplying their needs. These include MELCO, Toshiba, NEC, Hitachi, Oki Electric, Fujitsu, Mitsubishi Precision Co. and Japan Electronic Computer Co. Japan's missile needs are supplied by a variety of companies, which include MHI, Mitsubishi Electric, and Toshiba. In a similar vein, Hitachi, Toshiba and the ubiquitous Mitsubishi handle Japan's nuclear needs.

The Japanese defense industry therefore differs in many important ways from Japan's export oriented industries. Because it is not allowed to export, it must depend on domestic orders. Because they lack a really large indigenous market and are debarred from exporting, these companies need to interact with foreign defense firms as much as they need to protect their domestic markets from them. Even heavy industries, traditionally the most conservative and nationalistic in Japan's industrial community, have been forced to move away from large national aerospace projects and toward increasingly profitable subcontracting work for their American competitors. This is particularly true of the aircraft industry, which, along with the weapons and ammunition sectors, is the most heavily dependent on defense procurement.

The logical result of depending on sub-contracting work is that, for all purposes, *kokusanka* cannot work. The forest of information will remain with the American companies, who are increasingly black-boxing the most critical elements of it. This being so, Japan's trees of knowledge can never blossom into the forest needed for wide scale unilateral military action. Therefore, unilateral action by Japan against China or some similar power is impossible under present conditions.

The fact that the defense industry plays such a small proportionate role in Japan's overall economic performance also mitigates against Japan remilitarizing. Times have changed from the 1894–95 war and Japan's industrial giants do not derive their strength from military procurements any more. The special case of the Korean War apart, the defense industry has not been an important component of overall GDP since the Pacific War. Even Mitsubishi

Heavy Industries is much less dependent on defense sales than its American competitors. This is important in two ways. It means that even those companies such as MHI, which depend most on defense procurement, do not regard it as vital to their survival. This is in contrast to their American rivals who will lobby hard to retain the sale of big-ticket items to Japan. Therefore, in any trade disputes between Japan and America, Japan will have to yield to America on issues pertaining to the defense industry. Secondly, *kokusanka* policies that disrupt the American alliance are particularly troublesome. America would see a revived *kokusanka* sector as costing them sales in Japan and further afield if these Japanese companies ever started to export their merchandise. This is all the more so as America is increasingly linking *kokusanka* to its spin-off benefits. Because America wishes to get some of the dual-use technologies Japan's defense-related industries have developed, defense is going to be increasingly related with commerce in the years to come. This will undermine the whole commercial rationale for *kokusanka*. If Japanese companies cannot even develop the dual-use technologies they need to break even on their production, why should they expend their resources on defensive weapons?

Exports would offer one solution. Japan, for example, has expressed an interest in the privatization of the Romanian defense industry—not perhaps the most prized of markets, but a market nonetheless. Although the Romanian Defense minister has had meetings with the Japan Defense Industry Association as well as separate ones with both MHI and KHI, the Japanese are unlikely to be successful. Japan's plans to create joint companies to produce non-lethal defense-related equipment are too indirect to be effective. Until such time as the export ban is lifted, plans such as these can only stutter along. Until national policy changes, *kokusanka* cannot depend on foreign sales.

Without foreign sales, *kokusanka* is too expensive and, therefore, ultimately untenable. Japan's F-2 trainer, for example, cost twelve times what an equivalent American plane would have cost.

Cost is not the only problem. The impact on the American alliance is a bigger one. The durability of the present alliance with America depends in large measure on Japan's willingness to accept dependence on the United States in the area of defense industrial capabilities and defense procurement. Japan must address this fundamental dilemma and find a way to escape from the twin dangers of entrapment and abandonment. Because the first principle of Japan's foreign policy must be never to allow the United States to become an adversary, Japan must develop a technological edge that enhances the alliance and Japan's role in it. This brings its own problems with it.

Increasingly, the United States has black-boxed sensitive software for fire control systems, missile guidance and flight control in aircraft. In order to repair such software, the JSDF must ship them to the United States where they receive lower priority than weaponry from NATO or America's allies in the Middle East. The license production agreements, that allow much of Japan's needs to be built in Japan, also extract a heavy price. The JDA believe that they are overcharged to offset America's own research and development costs.

The whole *kokusanka* debate has, by and large, been an unhappy one from Japan's point of view. The *kokusanka* debate began at the time of the Korean War when MHI developed the F-86 Saber jet. Japan was trying to use defense contracts like the F-86 to launch a commercial aircraft industry and, if possible, a presence in the military aerospace industry as well. Because MHI could not depend on large and sustained orders for the F-86 or the F-104, which succeeded it, they had to look at possible spin-off uses instead. Japan's current plans to produce supersonic jets and to develop an early warning radar system suffer from the same problems. The orders are just not there to justify the expenses involved. The use of commercial spin-offs is therefore the Holy Grail of the Japanese arms industry.

The development of smart weapons has complicated the issue

by bringing new companies like Toshiba and MELCO to the core of Japan's defense industry. Although the entry of these companies into the market brought some much-needed competition with them, they also highlighted some of the outmoded and ultimately self-defeating structures of Japanese industry. MELCO, for example, would not share information with its close *keiretsu* ally MHI, as both companies competed to produce the Badge early warning system and the Nike/Hawk surface-to-air missile in the mid 1970s. These new companies are changing the industry. They do not depend on defense for any significant portion of their profits. They will abandon the sector if circumstances warrant it. More generally, when taken into the overall context of Japan's industrial and military links with America, they again tend to undermine the viability of *kokusanka* and, therefore, the possibility of Japan sustaining autonomous actions in a hot war.

The *kokusanka* movement had its upside. It began the quest in earnest for civilian spin-offs and away from having an autonomous arms industry. This was the beginning of Japan playing to its own technological strengths, not those of America. The focus on subsystems-level *kokusanka* was ideal for the growing number of Japanese electronics firms engaged in defense production. It is here that many of Japan's comparative advantages in the field now lie. The ASM-1, for example, was designed and built in the 1970s in Japan. During tests, it hit 28 out of 29 targets, proving its superiority to both the French-made Exocet and the British Harpoon, which figured prominently in the Falklands War of the early 1980s. Japan's expertise, as already has been pointed out, has proved world class in smart bombs. Much of that can be attributed to the spin-off benefits in opto-electronics.

These Japanese gains also brought their own costs with them, most notably in the howls of protests that came from the American defense industry and its allies on Capitol Hill. The late 1970s also saw the first sustained American requests for Japan to share its technology with them. These requests developed into the massive argument over the FSX project. The FSX was an over-ambitious project with the military objective of allowing Japan to develop a counter to the growing regional threat of Soviet air superiority. Although the Soviets were one pressing problem, they were not the only one. Japan's defense industry wanted to use it as a launching pad to develop a state-of-the-art Japanese plane that could win significant civilian orders as well as fulfilling its military requirements. Japanese companies were already developing some features that would help in this regard. These included composite wing materials, phased array radar, air-to-surface missiles, surface-to-air missiles and Controlled Configured Vehicle (CCVV) systems. They thought they could develop these individual trees of knowledge into the required forest if the U.S. helped in a subsidiary role.

The Japanese had already been "growing" quite a lot of different trees and putting them all, by quiet degrees, into one package that they hoped would allow them to enter the cutting edge of the aerospace industry. That one package was the T-4 Trainer. The XT-4 was Japan's first design-to-cost aircraft. The jet was finished on time, meeting or surpassing all mission specifications and at a fifth of the cost of America's equivalent, the aborted T-46 trainer project. The XT-4 had an indigenous turbofan. It also had a significant amount of composite materials from Japan's research into carbon fibers. It was clearly something to be proud of.

Although the XT-4 was a top-class trainer plane, there is a world of difference between fighters and trainers. These include the difference between Japan's F-3 engine and the front-line engines American companies produced. It also used a lot of American avionics, causing American critics to later claim that the FSX was an American plane in all but name.

The Americans, conscious of the potential loss of market share, took up this call. They pointed to the SH-X antisubmarine helicopter, which they claimed was only a modified version of the world-renowned, U.S.-made SH-60 Seahawk. They were not going to allow the Japanese to do any more intellectual poaching. At stake was the technological destiny of the aerospace industries of Japan and America. The American companies charged that their Japanese counterparts in the FSX project were in reality using an American prototype to develop an alternative Japanese plane that would push America out of its traditional markets.

At the same time as this controversy was raging, other developments rattled the Americans. Although Japan's companies were then conquering all before them, the American defense industry had been immune from their acquisitions. Fujitsu then made an offer for Fairchild, one of America's leading semiconductor companies with major defense contracts. And Toshiba illegally sold top American secrets to the Soviet navy, which enabled the latter to evade America's radar surveillance. Japan's trade surpluses with America continued to soar to unprecedented levels, Toshiba was selling American technology to America's Soviet enemies, Fujitsu were taking over key parts of the American defense industry and now they wanted the technology of their best fighter planes. America's demagogues jumped on the debate, the inevitable comparisons with Pearl Harbor were churned out and the FSX joint project floundered.

The long drawn out FSX debacle exhausted the patience of American companies, which saw the FSX being an American plane in all but name. They felt that they were being cheated and, that if they allowed the project to go through, the Japanese would eventually eclipse them in the entire industry. They regarded the entire FSX project as a Japanese attempt to leapfrog into the cutting edge of the industry by basing the FSX on an existing U.S. jet and engine. They were having none of it.

Though less vociferous, the Japanese were quite annoyed themselves with the whole debacle. America poached a lot of Japanese technology from the JSX project. These acquisitions included MHI's highly cost-effective technique for manufacturing the gallium arcenide-based modules for the plane's radar system. Because MHI can produce this at a fraction of the cost of American companies, this has led to savings of billions of dollars as the U.S. upgrades its fighter planes. Although this was an exceptional case, there were many other notable trees of Japanese knowledge that are now part of the American forest. These include MELCO's active phased radar technology, which they would have preferred to black-box. Indeed, America's insistence on a whole array of flow-back technology, that is access to Japanese technology in such areas as gallium arcenide chips, co-cured composite wings and phased array radar, made the Japanese extremely reluctant to get into any future major joint products with their erstwhile allies.

The FSX debate was, therefore, an important forerunner of the current TMD debate. The TMD entails Japan abandoning not only its *kokusanka* option but it also demands it surrenders its commercial technological assets to the U.S. defense industry. It thereby brings the old argument of entrapment versus abandonment into the modern era. The sheer size of the program ensures that. TMD's proposed $10 billion price tag would dwarf everything else in Japan's defense budget. The immediate risk is that Japan's defense budgets would be so financially drained by their purchase of an untested off-the-shelf American system that they would not have the financial resources to maintain their other defense needs. The TMD is simply too large to allow for a credible Japanese alternative. Japan's defense would remain, to all intents and purposes, in the hands of the Pentagon.

So too would a large section of Japan's cutting edge industrial expertise. The technology for technology (TFT) proposals, which are an integral part of the TMD proposals, ask Japan to do something it cannot do: deliver commercial technology from firms reluctant to do so. Firms such as Kyocera and Sharp, which have the technology the Pentagon desires, are not interested in TFT or, indeed, the good graces of MITI or the JDA for that matter. Defense is a minuscule part of the overall business of the Japanese firms with the most desirable technologies. MHI, KHI and the other firms with the most exposure to the defense sector have the least amount of technological secrets to offer. The important firms in the middle—firms like MELCO, NEC, and Hitachi—which have some technological cookies all depend on defense procurement for less than three percent of their business. Their dual-use technologies will remain firmly black-boxed for the foreseeable future.

There is another dimension to all of this. Although Japan's indigenous defense technology, based on the application of advanced civilian technology, has proved highly effective and is now being emulated in the United States, all-embracing military systems are just becoming too expensive and complicated for autonomous development by powers such as Japan.

Europe's experiences exemplify. Although Mitsubishi has done some minor joint ventures with Daimler Aerospace and although British Aerospace has sold BAE-125 aircraft to the JDA in recent years, these do not lessen Japan's dependence on the United States at all. The global industry is contracting. Even Boeing and McDonnell Douglas are finding it tough and the Europeans have been forced to come together to develop their Eurofighter. The Eurofighter project, which involves most of Europe's leading aerospace and electronics firms, has had to overcome vast obstacles to become a reality. These include Britain's purchases of rival American planes, the self-interest of the French and Swedish firms not directly involved in the project, and a viable formula to divide the costs, profits, and technological secrets among the various firms involved.

Japan cannot hope to present a unilateral, credible challenge to the American and European aerospace and avionics industries. It must develop systems suitable for its own needs. The next chapter looks at Japan in some detail to ascertain what those needs actually are.

Japan's Home Front

Religious fanatics unleashed sarin nerve-gas canisters against Japanese subway commuters on March 20, 1995. The attack, timed for maximal effect during Tokyo's morning rush hour, left 12 people dead and seriously injured 5,000 more. Sarin gas, being the devilish remnant of the Great War that it is, meant that the deaths were slow and agonizing. The injuries were equally horrific. One woman had to have both eyes surgically removed. Other survivors had their insides destroyed by the poisonous fumes. Japan stood horrified—and afraid.

The police quickly identified the perpetrators as members of a prominent doomsday religious group called Aum Shinri Kyo, the Aum Divine Truth Sect*. Shoko Asahara, the sect's tubby guru, was convicted in 2004, but a death sentence was postponed pending further investigations into the activities of the sect. In the

---

* Aum have an award-winning site at Aum: http://aum-internet.org/. For those interested in cults in general, good information is to be found at: http://www. rickross.com/

meantime, his foot soldiers remain at large, recruiting more followers to unleash their venom on Japan and on the world. These threats cannot be easily dismissed simply because the ringleaders have been rounded up—and, hopefully, the keys to their cells thrown away. Police and army raids subsequent to the attack uncovered several hundred tons of toxic chemicals in Aum-controlled warehouses. These guys had enough sarin gas ingredients stockpiled to kill over 4 million people.

More worrying still, the police raids uncovered evidence that Aum was also experimenting with biological agents, and even building nuclear weapons. Aum was particularly interested in the use of ebola, smallpox, yellow fever, botulism, and aflatoxin bacteria as potential biological warfare agents. If these lethal cocktails were not surreal enough, police unearthed evidence that Aum were also developing a technique for enriching uranium using laser beam equipment.

Because Japan cannot eliminate the threat this small but crazy group poses, this chapter has to question her ability to deal with the much stronger danger her neighbors North Korea, China, or Russia could pose. Aum put on the pretense of being an oppressed religious minority and demand the freedom to organize themselves as they see fit. The fact that they pose a threat to the rest of Japanese society does not faze them. Their dastardly deeds notwithstanding, they demand their religious rights. And Japan finds it hard to refuse.

Aum's tactic plays on many of Japan's latent insecurities. Because Imperial Japan persecuted to the point of extinction its religious minorities, the Occupation forces made religious tolerance one of the hallmarks of the post-war Japanese system. The Japanese authorities agreed. And they got lumbered with the nerve gas attack of Aum, itself a bizarre blend of Shintoism and other Eastern and Western religions.

Aum, if not built on the flimsiest of foundations, was certainly centered on the unlikeliest of gurus. Matsumoto Chizuo, Asahara as he styles himself, was the cult's tubby, shortsighted leader. When he was six, he was sent to a school for the blind, where he remained incarcerated for the next fourteen years. As a young all-but-blind man in the late 1970s, he supported himself, his wife and his many mistresses by selling counterfeit medicine. Having got repeatedly arrested for such lowly scams, he decided to find himself a new career. He established Aum Shinsen No Kai (God's Prophets) in 1984 and later changed his name to Asahara Shoko to give himself a more esoteric appeal. Returning from an information-gathering exercise in the Himalayas, where he had the opportunistic foresight to have his picture taken with the Dalai Lama, he changed the name of his cult to Aum Shinikyou, The Church of Supreme Truth. He was quickly rewarded, for in August 1989 Aum Shinrikyou was recognized as a religion for tax relief purposes by the Japanese authorities. Armed with pictures of his eminent self taken with the Dalai Lama and other staples from his con man days, the recruits and the money rolled in.

Heavy-handed tactics also helped Aum's bottom line considerably. On November 4, 1989, Aum kidnapped lawyer Tsutsumi Sakamoto, who had been one of their most outspoken critics. They murdered Sakamoto, his wife, and his one-year-old baby boy, and then dismembered them before burying them in unmarked graves. In June 1994, Aum unleashed sarin gas near an apartment where another anti-Aum lawyer was living. Eight people in nearby apartments died. Later, in February 28, 1995, Kiyoshi Kariya, another anti-Aum lawyer, was murdered. Aum atomized him in a giant microwave they had specially constructed for such purposes and dumped his bones into a lake. The following month, on March 20, 1995, they unleashed sarin gas on five different Tokyo trains with the devastating results already described. Ten days later, on March 30, Aum shot Police Commissioner Takaji Kunimatsu in an effort to stop his investigations into the murders. They were unsuccessful, and on May 16 Japan breathed a sigh of relief. Asahara, Mr. Tubby, was arrested.

The reign of terror had ended. For the time being. The subway arrests merely put their plans on hold. Plans, which included spraying nerve gas over Tokyo from helicopters they had specially secured for that very purpose, were put on hold—not abandoned. There is no sign of Aum disintegrating. Members remain free to practice their devotions—and to recruit many more dupes to their fanatical ranks. Although plans are afoot to strip Aum of its remaining assets, they are a resilient and resourceful bunch, who will not be easily deterred. They will be back. Their target recruiting pond, Japan's alienated cognitive elite, will see to that. So too will Aum's resources.

Aum's war chest is being topped up by the proceeds of public lectures and concerts, Internet sales of audiocassettes, T-shirts, and other official cult paraphernalia. Six AUM discount computer stores generate sales of more than $61 million a year. Trisal Computer, a discount computer store in the heart of Tokyo's Electric City district, typifies these ventures. Despite its infamy as an Aum front, a constant stream of computer nerds find their way into its clutches. They are drawn in by Trisal's low prices, its catchy websites, and the flyers passed out by Aum's pretty foot soldiers. Aum's software engineers have even designed security systems for the Japanese defense forces. Aum, in other words, seems to be a more potent adversary than the rest of Japan put together.

Although, at the time of writing, the Japanese government has moved to confiscate Aum's computer stores, Aum have vowed to reopen them. Aum are still far from out. The "Wanted" mug shots of their top guns still adorn every subway station and police station in Tokyo and they still conduct the occasional kidnap of dissidents or potential police informers. As Aum are also trying to incorporate under a variety of different names, we can be sure that Asahara's top lieutenants are in it for the long haul. The group, which apologised to the victims and admitted its involvement for the first time in December 1999, has been trying to distance itself in the public's eye from the past. It has most recently changed its name to Aleph, renounced Shoko Asahara as their guru and said it would close down its computer companies, which earned it millions of dollars. In March 2000, on the fifth anniversary of the attack, the cult issued its first formal apology for the attacks. However, just two months later, police found detailed instructions for making nerve gas in a car owned by the cult, leading officials to suspect the group may have been planning to resume production of the poison. According to subsequent reports in the Japanese media, the cult is now trying to revive itself with a drive to recruit new members. If Japan cannot handle this small group, what hope have they against North Korea?

Though Asahara remains incarcerated, he has not forgotten his troops. He is telling his army to prepare for Armageddon. Given the diabolical arsenal that Aum had assembled, Asahara clearly intends Aum to play a central part in the mayhem Armageddon portends. Asahara, oddly enough given his track record, sees himself at the center of this coming conflict. This, on reflection, is not that surprising, given that he thinks he is Jesus, God the Father and the Holy Spirit combined—combined with an ocean-wide streak of malevolence. Because he has not forgotten them, Asahara's dupes have not forgotten him. Aum's web pages have proclaimed Asahara's prison a "sacred training place." About 170 Aum diehards have settled near the detention house and have unsettled the locals in the process. Local property values have plunged. Local real estate investors are not alone in their fears. The cult has never apologized or renounced its doctrine of attaining enlightenment through mass murder. Concern over the cult isn't limited to Japan: The U.S. State Department lists Aum on its roster of terrorist organizations. The United States was their ultimate target. The United States remains their ultimate target.

The Aum example is particularly interesting because of the insights it provides into the wider Japanese society, the focus of this chapter. Aum appealed to the worst elements of Japanese nationalism and, in the process, they attracted Japan's brightest, graduates of her top universities, all honored and esteemed members of her cognitive elite, to her shadowy ranks. Aum's organizational structure helped to do the rest. Beneath the bells and the tambourines, the robes and the religious façade, Aum had a deadlier purpose—and an organization structured to achieve its purpose. Aum, like similar quasi-religious organizations in the West, erected insurmountable boundaries between themselves and the outside world. Once a group as socially isolated as Aum decides to accept a leader's authority, there are no real mechanisms for providing checks or balances on their abuses of power, or even of giving an alternative to the leader's interpretation of events, for that would entail challenging the leader's imposed consensus. Japan, because of its lack of a democratic tradition, is particularly vulnerable in this respect. It is simply not geared for the types of sustained campaigns of violence Aum had planned.

Kimitake Hiraoka, who wrote award-winning novels under the pseudonym of Mishima Yukio, tried to do something similar to Aum some years earlier. Mishima also had his own nutty samurai army, the Shield Society. He too wanted to reinvigorate Japan, to abandon Article 9 of the Constitution, to reawaken its martial spirits and, samurai sword in hand, to let Japan cut a swathe through the international community and thereby gain its rightful place at the helm of history. To achieve this dubious goal, Mishima and four of his sidekicks invaded the Japanese army's headquarters in Tokyo on November 25, 1970 and took a few hostages, whereupon Mishima committed ritual suicide. This silly act did not impress Mishima's target audience. The onlookers, drawn from Japan's modern defense forces, reckoned he was insane. Ritual suicide held no attractions for them and Mishima's efforts to galvanize them only ended in farce.

Japan's right wing organizations are equally farcical. These groups expend their time and energies driving around Tokyo in menacing convoys of large black trucks, blaring out martial music and imploring Japan's citizens to return to the imperialist ways of the past. Japan's citizens are, by and large, only annoyed by their noisy intrusions. The megaphones are particularly loud and as grating on the ear as their large trucks are displeasing to the eye. These people cut little ice with the population at large, who have their own more mundane concerns to see to.

That said, these fringe groups do form a very discernible threat. It is, however, a terrorist threat, a threat from the outside of the main fabric of life. In that, they are fundamentally different from the military terrorism, which galvanized Japan in the inter-war years. These groups are the product of the alienated margins, not of the mainstream. Therefore, though they do present a threat, and a particularly obnoxious one at that, they do not currently present a fundamental threat to the fabric of Japanese life. The basic fabric of post-war Japan sees to that. Therefore, the Aum threat is mainly a useful prism to view the overall threats Japan faces and the dangers a reformed Japan present.

Aum is what results when millennial cults are given space to organize and recruit. Although the Aum attack had religious elements to it, the threat was peripheral to the main run of affairs. Although well educated, motivated and armed, they are an isolated threat only to the margins of Japanese society. This does not make them less dangerous: it just means that their threats will remain localized as long as the center holds. And this chapter goes on to show how conservatively resilient is the center of Japanese political life.

Though incarcerated, Shoko Asahara remains a particularly dangerous man—a dangerous living god, if Aum is to be believed. Asahara had his followers convinced that indiscriminate mass murder would through "poa"—a Tibetan Buddhist term for reincarnation to a higher existence—be good for them. He convinced them that they would rejuvenate their bodies in this world and save their souls in the next by committing mass murder. More incredibly, his followers were dumb enough to believe him. Asahara had convinced many of Japan's most intelligent citizens that he was the living incarnation of God, and that mass murder and indiscriminate nerve gas attacks were, if done in homage to him, religious, pious and holy acts. And they believed him!

Although Aum's plot seems like a particularly threadbare James Bond thriller, it was fact, not fiction. Nor was there any James Bond to nip them in the bud, to head them off at the pass. Quite the reverse in fact. Aum had admirers and followers galore in the academic and intelligence communities and the degree to which they can reactivate that support will determine how lethal a threat they can present in the future. Japan's social and economic structures make that unlikely. They make Aum too far divorced from the mainstream of Japanese life to allow it to gain critical popular mass.

Although Aum conjures up a vision of demented Japanese scientists committing mass murder with gay abandon, that is a distorted view. It just imposes Western ways of analyzing society onto Japan, which is fundamentally different in so many key respects from the major nations of the West. Japan just does not fit into the simpler democratic models of, say, the United States with its Republican and Democratic parties, or Britain with its Labour and Tory parties. Only Israel has an equivalent of Soka Gakkai, the lay Buddhist group that can muster nearly seven million votes, 10 percent of Japan's total. Aum's apologists have repeatedly tried to blame Soka Gakkai for their own outrages and have instanced Soka Gakkai's lucrative contracts with the Mainichi press group as evidence of their culpability. Aum's longer-term tactic was to hijack the political and spiritual space Soka Gakkai, Sukyo Mahikari and similar groups hold in modern Japan. The trouble with this is that these organizations are fundamentally different from Aum. Although they all have spiritual dimensions to them, Soka Gakkai is simply a richer and better connected Japanese equivalent of the Salvation Army. It is firmly in the conservative mainstream and has nothing to gain by associating with Aum or using its terrorist tactics. Like Israel, most of Japan's religious zealots are ultimately harmless. Aum's propaganda notwithstanding, Soka Gakkai is on the harmless side of the spectrum. All the violence in the world will not transform such groups into rampaging zealots. They are more concerned with overcharging for the burial plots they control than with sparking the next world war. Though Aum may bark all they like, they will never be able to take over this conservative mainstream.

Although groups such as Soka Gakkai can hold the balance of power in the fragile democracy that is Japan, they do not present the threat denominational zealots present in the West or the Middle East. This is because, in general, the Japanese are not zealots. America's atomic bombs put a permanent end to that era. Japan's religious beliefs are now of a different order. They are, by and large, secondary to the more immediate question of surviving in the pressure cooker of modern Japanese life. Aum and organizations like them are merely symptoms of the quest for something deeper. The generally pluralistic nature of modern Japan ensures that such searches will bypass dangerous groups like Aum. No more than America or any other modern society can Japan hope to eliminate them altogether. As long as the Japanese people exist, they will strive to put meanings on their lives. Some of them will look for meaning in the wrong places—by joining organizations headed by outcasts like Asahara and Mishima. These people and the groups they spawn will always exist. The best that can be done is to disarm them—and marginalize them into irrelevance.

Aum and Mishima are merely the Japanese manifestations of the worldwide problems of decadence and alienation, of the spiritual need of the flock for a leader, and of the leader for immortality. Because Japan is not the West, these people and the groups they spawn just do not have direct Western equivalents. Japan just does not fit comfortably into our Western models of how societies run. Indeed, if a Western comparison was needed, the Weimar Republic of Germany's inter-war years might be as appropriate a model as any other.

Modern Japan can at least match it in certain branches of decadence. *Enjo Kosai*†, a system whereby young schoolgirls prostitute themselves, has taken sex-crazed Tokyo by storm. Up to eight percent of all schoolgirls regularly work as comfort women, in order to buy the expensive consumer goods Tokyo's material world demands. Because there's no poverty or drugs involved and the deal is consensual between the Lolitas and their clients, the police merely take their names and notify the comfort girl's unconcerned parents of the somewhat personal commercial transaction they have uncovered. Japan's age of consent was 12 until very recently when foreign outrage forced the politicians to raise the age to a nominal 18. Although a new law criminalizes having sex with minors with up to one year in prison and a $4000 fine, only a few Japanese businessmen have been busted so far for having paid sex with the *Loli-chans*, and this is probably more of a "face-saving" gesture than a genuine crackdown. Not that a wide-scale clampdown would be all plain sailing. There is trenchant opposition to clamping down on the *Loli-chan* industry. Opponents of stronger child-sex laws include the Communist Party, several teachers' unions and even mothers' groups who remember their own cash-starved school days.

Japan, to reiterate, is different from the West. Even on this basic question of pedophilia, we find a fundamental divide, which inhibits action. A large minority of Japanese people avails of the services these children provide. Their interests revolve around such things, not around the hassles and discomforts foreign conquests and disputes entail. They just could not be bothered upsetting the status quo. Other, equally large and more conservative swathes of Japanese society want to make sure that their daughters do not

---

† *Enjo* means "aid" and *Kosai* means "acquaintance." Literally, the term means "compensated dating" whereby an older man gives a schoolgirl money to buy teenage things in exchange for a date. Because the date usually ends up in a love hotel, the term is really a euphemism for child prostitution.

use *enjo kosai* as a gateway into Japan's vast criminal netherworld. They tend to be over-protective or, if you will, ultra-conservative in their views. Overseas conquests are not for them either.

Japan is not, in other words, as decadent as the hyped-up *enjo kosai* craze might suggest. Japanese society has a large, socially conservative streak at its core. The oral contraceptive pill, for example, was only legalized in 1999—the last major country to legalize it. Viagra, meanwhile, the pill that reinvigorates the manhood of older men, was also legalized in 1999—after only six weeks. The reasons reflect Japanese society. It is a socially conservative country, where the needs of older men are given precedence. Thus, the fast lane for Viagra—and the much slower one for the pill. Japan's large medical profession successfully opposed the introduction of the pill for decades: they were making so much money from providing abortion services that they feared a substantial drop in income if the pill was introduced. Socially conservative groups, like Japan's medical profession, do not form the backbone of overseas military adventures. They are too selfish and self-centered and, as Viagra suggests, simply too old.

There are other important examples of Japan's social conservatism worth noting. The earthquake in Kobe in January 1995, for example, was unique among modern calamities in that there was no looting. Quite the opposite in fact. It led to an outpouring of volunteer action unprecedented in Japan. Over 1 million volunteers combined their efforts and donated over 100 billion-yen to disaster relief. This shows a Japanese public more concerned with acts of charity and goodwill than campaigns of conquest. But Kobe was also only the most dramatic expression of the Japanese government's incapacity to function in a whole range of areas. These include not only the Aum outrage, but also scandals over tainted blood and the financial and criminal scandals detailed in *Japan's Big Bang*. The government's lethargy would suggest that normal Japanese society is breaking down. The need seems to lie in concentrating on decentralizing the trappings of power, of allowing non-government organizations to fill up the social space a central-izing, hierarchical political system cannot.

Indeed, the local Japanese *yakuza* were the first to offer an organized and effective response to the Kobe earthquake, further evidence that Japan is not a normal Western-style democracy. The *yakuza* and right wing pressure groups have been quite important allies of the governing LDP and other conservative groupings since 1945. Yoshio Kodama, a major post-war criminal figure, funded the political campaigns of Ichiro Hatoyama and Nobosuke Kishi, both of whom became prime ministers of Japan in the 1950s. However, although the *yakuza* are over-indulged, again this does not tell the full story. Despite these dark shadows, Japan is not an authoritar-ian society. It is merely lethargically corrupt and somewhat bureaucratic in its approach to matters such as these.

And, although corruption is endemic, Japan has prospered, grown and changed out of all recognition from the time of its defeat in the Pacific War. This economic growth has made it politi-cally stable as well. Since the war, Japan has been a country of almost unique political stability. One party has ruled it for thirty-eight unbroken years. This single conservative party, the Liberal Democratic Party, won almost every national election and most local contests from 1955 up to the present. They thereby set a pat-tern that will be very resistant to change for many years yet. They made Japanese politics very predictable, even mundane but at the same time, they achieved wholesale social and economic change without the serious political disruptions that affected Italy, France, South Korea and many other countries during the same years.

This complacency has become so entrenched in the Japanese mindset that, the efforts of Aum and Mishima notwithstanding, it will be almost impossible to change. The only changes Japan can expect will be incremental, marginal and pragmatic. Any study of Japanese society in its various manifestations leads to that same conclusion.

The Japanese mindset has been conditioned over the post-war

years to accept some things as fixed and immutable. These include its economic, military, and social links with America. Any major contraction of these links would be a veritable tidal wave in the sea of tranquillity that is modern political Japan. This is the model that has been in effect since 1955, the so-called 1955 system. This system embedded the LDP as the majority party in the Diet and divided it from its opposition on such major ideological issues as foreign policy, general security, and constitutional reform. These issues have now been largely fought and won. The American link is secure, the constitution preaches non-violence and, eccentric folk like Mishima notwithstanding, that can only be marginally and incrementally changed. Japan is not going to suddenly embark on any maverick overseas military adventure. They are not suddenly going to clash with Russia or China over their territorial disputes. Their future path will merely reflect their approach since 1955. In general, it will be slow and cautious and it will favor the checkbook over the stick.

Japan's bureaucrats will see to that. The LDP has been closely linked to a traditionally strong bureaucracy and major interest groups have aligned themselves with relevant government ministries and their bureaucracies. Political life was orderly under these arrangements and the dominant characteristic was one of hierarchy and deference. Although the Finance Ministry has lost much of its power in recent years, the overall conservative and cautious approach remains. There will be no major or radical change there for the foreseeable future. There have, of course, been some hiccups in the system in recent years. This was most obviously the case in 1993, when the LDP suffered from a wave of defectors, who subsequently formed a rival political party. The Japanese system seemed to have broken down. Splinter groups had peeled away from the LDP to form their own parties. The question we ask is, do these hiccups provide a threat to the status quo and the foreign policies it spawns?

The answer is no. Japan is a large and populous country where policy divisions have to be expected between different economic groupings as a matter of course. The well-known Japanese quest for consensus is as much an attempt to deal internally with such disputes as it is a reflection of some generically ethnic or cultural predisposition to mutual tolerance. The recent splits in the LDP were merely smaller manifestations of this longer-term trend to internalize divisions in what remains a very conservative country. The Japanese do not have as much a predisposition to consensus as they have a preference to keep their arguments private. Being conservatives, they are ill disposed to showing their dirty linen to the public at large.

When the Occupation ended, Japan was run by a coalition of conservative groupings, who had to find a *modus vivendi* between themselves. Colored by Japan's recent imperialist history and the subsequent territorial conquests of the Soviet Red Army and of the Chinese People's Liberation Army, many of these people and groupings wanted Japan to rearm and to adopt a more forthright stance in the region. Nobusuke Kishi, who propounded this line, lost the PM's job largely as a result of his hawkish stand. The fears that Japan would cast a longer shadow in the area led to Japan's biggest post-war demonstrations at the beginning of the 1960s—when the baby boomers born soon after the war were entering their university years.

These people had no desire to emulate their uncles and return to Japan in body bags. They were an important obstacle to Japan remilitarizing. So, too, was the impressive political machine the LDP was building. As these students were protesting, the LDP were solidifying their links with small business and small farmers, important social groups who outlived the demographic bubble of the 1960s and are still as vocally conservative today as they were then. The interests of these groups tend overwhelmingly toward protectionism and other manifestations of ultra conservatism.

Because of the exodus to the cities, the rural population has aged considerably—and old farmers make poor rebels. Compared with the imperial era, there are fewer farmers, they are older and they now derive much of their income from blue-collar work beyond the farm gate. These all shape their political views, which are overwhelmingly selfish and conservative. Their main campaigns have been for government price subsidies and assistance programs and against liberalization of imports. These are not the things agrarian revolutions are made of.

Rice is a good example. It takes about $2,000 to produce a ton of unhulled rice in Japan. In the United States, it can be done for less than $250 and in Thailand, a little over $100 would secure you your ton. The law of comparative advantage tells us that Japan should concentrate on what it can do cheaply—producing LCD televisions for example—and import what other countries have a comparative advantage in—rice, for example. The law of comparative advantage may tell us that. Japan's farmers sing a different tune. They have been implacable in their resistance to rice imports and other commodities, where Japan clearly lacks the competitive edge. They justify their appeals with a range of conservative arguments. These arguments have centered on the centrality of rice and other agricultural commodities to the very notion of Japan itself. The logic of their argument is that they should be paid twenty times the amount Indonesian or Thai farmers are paid for producing the same product. Cut to their core, these arguments are reactionary and isolationist. Some of them, such as the one Ysutomu Hata, an LDP defector who founded the Renewal Party, which argued for restricting the import of American beef on the grounds that the Japanese have longer intestines, are simply silly. All of them, however, are conservative. In the final analysis, a country that subsidizes its farmers to the extent that Japan does cannot be dynamic in its foreign policy. It is too protectionist for today's information age and will lose any propaganda wars this stance entails. Any bold stand by Japan will lead to a cackle of derisory protests from its trading partners on everything from the length of Japanese intestines and the unique features of Japanese snow to the extortionate price of Japanese rice.

The same arguments pertain even more forcefully to the powerful retail sector. Japan is characterized by a preponderance of very small and very expensive stores—more than twice the ratio of the United States. This group has been largely successful in delaying the introduction of supermarkets into Japan. The entire distributional network is only one of Japan's many hidden taxes. They reap more from imported alcohol, for example, than the government collects in taxes. They also explain why Japanese tourists go on buying binges when they hit the malls of Singapore, Hong Kong, Europe, and the United States. When compared to Tokyo, even the most expensive overseas boutiques are cheap.

It is not as much a question of shop till you drop as shop till you go home and face Japan's vast and largely superfluous distribution system. Though it might be superfluous to today's needs, this army of retailers and wholesalers has proved incredibly resilient and well organized. They have therefore been able to command high degrees of political support for their largely reactionary agenda of keeping themselves in business by bleeding the Japanese consumer dry. Consumer groups have proved ineffective in the face of their stance—and that of Japanese food producers. The same goes for Japan's high utility rates, which are due in large part to the subsidies Japan's coal industry receives. Japan's consumers meekly pay up. They are part of the cozy apple cart of modern Japan and they will be very slow to upset their place in it.

The entire picture is one of sluggish reaction, of stagnant conservatism, where artificially high prices keep large and reactionary business constituencies happy. Japan is not pre-revolutionary Iran, where the farmers and small retailers were driven into rebellion by the Shah's economic policies. Japan is nearly the polar opposite of the Shah's Iran. The farmers enjoy a very high standard of living when compared to their urban compatriots. They are, in the main, an aging and conservative rump, which will be marginalized, if at all, by small, incremental and time-consuming steps.

The same applies to the small retailers, who know that they have to hang together if they do not want to hang separately. They will continue to impede progress and, in the process, ensure that Japan is not engulfed by radicalism of any political hue.

The LDP funnels all of these reactionary and conservative groups into its own vast, political camp. These large but localized pressure groups reflect the broader stratum of Japanese society who keep the LDP in power. These Japanese voters tend to be dis-interested in national politics. Theirs is a mixture of the pork bar-rel and the Sony Walkman. As long as their living standards can be maintained and as long as Sony and similar companies make their long commutes to and from work bearable, they will not complain too much. Nor will the LDP, who are the biggest benefi-ciaries of this system.

The LDP's roots run deep. They are heirs to a long tradition of conservative rule in Japan. In spite of the development of some centralized political and economic institutions, modern Japanese political power remains decentralized and parochial in many key ways. Japan has roughly double the amount of small retail and wholesale outlets that America has. Not only that but Japanese firms in general tend to be much smaller than their American or West European counterparts. This means that small-scale capital-ists and their employees are much more important in Japan than in the West. This being so, their social and political horizons tend to be much narrower. Their political leaders will reflect their views and concerns on protectionism and the like. Because Japan is among the world's largest economies, this will not change in the foreseeable future. The sociology of Japan's economy has been set in an immutably conservative mold.

The political structure of Japan is therefore overwhelmingly conservative. It depends on hierarchical groups striking deals between their factions and mobilizing the masses to fall into line at election time. The network of informal associations crisscrossing Japanese social life underscores this fundamental conservatism.

The LDP has an entire machine under it, which excludes only labor unions and religious organizations, the two bodies most likely to offer dual political loyalties.

Mobilization is also a crucial factor in Japanese politics, which further underscores its conservative heart. Successful Japanese politicians almost invariably have particularly powerful local party machines. The most notorious of these, Kakuei Tanaka's Etsuzanki's organization, had 315 municipal assemblymen, 26 mayors and 11 prefectural assemblymen lined up behind him in Niigata. This gives a strong regional input into the Diet. It also gives politicians an almost omnipotent hold on the local scene. Clearly, little was going to happen in Tanaka's Niigata backyard to unsaddle him. The same scenario is repeated throughout the entire archipelago. Conservatism is cemented into the entire country's political structures at every level.

From Hokkaido in the far north to Okinawa in the deep south, networks of conservative groupings maintain the fabric of Japanese political society. Over 40 million Japanese voters are enrolled in political support groups of one sort or another. In other words, the votes of over half of the entire electorate can be counted on before polling even begins. And the Diet members cast a sufficiently wide and comprehensive net to boost that percentage to even higher, unassailable levels. Tanaka's last such event was to give a free weekend holiday to 110,000 constituents. The large amount of public works projects also keeps local support high among constituents and the businesses, which get the contracts. Japan, in short, can expect no backwoods revolt. Unlike America with its talk radios, its militias, its ethnic divisions and its ensuing tensions, Japan is homogeneous and tranquil. The voice of dissent cannot gain a foothold to nibble away at the societal consensus, which underwrites the LDP. Mishima and Asahara are not the only ones pushed to the margins. Anything, which threatens the political status quo, shares a similar fate.

The LDP, as a de facto alliance, has always had its strains. These climaxed when the party kingpin and the party's most accomplished manipulator, Shin Kanemaru, was arrested in a bribery probe and a fortune in gold bars was discovered in his house. His fall from grace was followed by major defections from the LDP in July 1993. The end result was that the LDP lost office for the first time since its formation. However, even the LDP's 1993 loss of power did not change Japan's overall political mold. Conservatives elements, which had defected from the LDP, remained prominent in the government. Though the government changed, little else did. As a consequence, the LDP quickly reasserted itself and soon regained power.

Japan just lacks any clear political cleavages to sustain instability. Although Komeito, the Clean Government Party, is sect-based and has a disciplined political following, religious issues are not contentious in Japanese politics. Indeed, almost nothing is. Japan is linguistically, ethnically, religiously, and regionally homogeneous for all practical purposes. It therefore lacks the necessary preconditions for internal instability, which these forces cause elsewhere in the world. Japan will therefore not become another Sri Lanka. Nor will it have the deep ideological divisions of the United States or France. Japan will remain overwhelmingly conservative and will not move out of the current alliance with the United States unless large external pressures force it to. Anybody waiting for radical change to emanate from within Japan will be in for a long and fruitless wait.

The ideological battles, such as they were, have all been fought and largely won by the big, conservative battalions. By far, the constitution has been the biggest ideological battleground of the last 50 years. By far, the most contentious part of the constitution has been the commitment to non-violence in international affairs. Although this is changing by incremental degrees, no sudden changes of major import can be expected on that front. Indeed, the debate has, as often as not, descended into the level of a French farce. The opposition socialist and communist parties, eager to show their pacifist tendencies, have nothing better to do with their time than object to Japanese teenagers waving the national flag and singing the national anthem at international soccer matches. It is unclear what they expect them to wave or sing instead. "The Star Spangled Banner" would hardly be appropriate and one would imagine that the Chinese would object to Japan commandeering their flag for international sporting occasions. And this is what the opposition parties preoccupy themselves with.

These pathetic protests notwithstanding, neither the national anthem nor the modern Japanese flag are liable to spark a revival in militarism. For most Japanese soccer fans, they are devoid of symbolic meaning and the opposition parties know that. Their protestations have a more pragmatic, if increasingly irrelevant spin to them. The constitution also gives labor the right to organize and the opposition's protests have as much to do with keeping their union supporters onside as it has with which national anthem is played on the country's karaoke machines. The opposition owe much of their support to the organized trade union movement. Although at least token opposition to the American alliance and a revival of Japanese militarism are parts of their beliefs, the rest of the fabric of Japanese political life tends to defang any momentum that could upset the alliance. The same forces guarantee the continued prominence of the LDP.

The LDP is as much a populist, if somewhat undemonstrative, party than a traditional conservative party. Although lacking the extroverted machismo of Mexico's PRI or Argentina's Peronistas, it has a vast and diverse grassroots support system, which even those parties would envy. The LDP's machine squeezes out all hopes of massive change in Japan's political status quo. The LDP's well-defined factional system also helps to keep things tranquil. There are generally between five and eight of these at any one time—as well as a large number of looser organizations that only further accentuate the trend toward political conservatism. Generally, these factions would all have a prominent senior LDP figure in charge. These groups are rarely if ever concerned with fundamental ideological issues. They are largely pragmatic groupings, more concerned with securing the spoils of office than with splitting over fundamental issues such as the American alliance.

Even though some of these factional leaders might have had strong views on security, the factions themselves rarely did. The pork barrel was their god. This being so, such issues have never been as contentious as they might otherwise have been. Nor were the factions at each other's throats. They were most likely instead at each other's ears, cutting deals to share the many perks of political office between themselves. The PM would usually be picked by a coalition of factions united along pragmatic not ideological grounds. Radicalism had no place to bloom in such a controlled system.

The Socialist Democratic Party of Japan was even more fractious. Their factions usually split along ideological lines and so ghettoized themselves and their beliefs as economic lift-off happened. Given that they were denied the plums of office, ideology was probably all they had to share between them. Now, all they can argue about is the color of flag supporters of the Japanese soccer team should wave.

Ideology has, in other words, become less important in Japanese politics as time has passed. Japan's rapid post-war growth has killed any chance of a major ideological rift. Japan rose from the ashes of defeat to build the world's second largest economy, a truly amazing and unique accomplishment. One argument then spins this achievement to say that, as the government directed this change, if a future government should so decide, Pearl Harbor and territorial expansion would happen all over again.

This argument is untenable. Faced with Japan's situational imperatives of late development, her lack of natural resources, her large population and her need to trade, the government and MITI did the only thing that they could do. With the help of their American allies, they built a formidable economy that became, to outside observers, a mere exporting machine. There is no doubt that Japan's impressive post-war performance did much to kill any major subversive radicalism that might otherwise have taken hold. However, if we accept this latter argument, then we must also accept that the sun is setting on Japan's economy. Japan is in decline.

Certainly, Japan's growth rates cannot continue. Per capita GNP has increased in nominal terms by a factor of 126 since 1945. Looking at it from a slightly longer vista, the twentieth century witnessed Japan being transformed from a relatively poor agricultural country to the world's second largest economy. Now, however, its key industries have peaked. Japan, in less than 40 years, has gone from being an insignificant producer of motor cars, to being the world's largest auto producer. Japan has been, in recent years, far and away the world's largest exporter of cars. That cannot continue. Nor can Japan make it continue. Japan certainly could not do it at the point of a bayonet. Japan cannot browbeat other countries into buying its products. Quite the reverse in fact. It must always fear the erection of protectionist walls. The same goes for consumer electronics, where Japanese exports again lead the world. There is a glut that Japan cannot solve except by internal restructuring. Economically, Japan must be on the defensive, not the offensive.

Japan's imports are likewise vulnerable. She imports nearly all of her oil, coal, iron, and copper. She is largely self-sufficient in rice and dairy products but imports most of her other foodstuffs. This comparative weakness again calls for defensive, not offensive actions. All of this must be reflected in defense policy.

Chapter
EIGHT

Into the Future

The Cold War was a period of international stasis. The Soviet Union and the United States, the world's two main political players during those years, shared sufficient common interests to avoid a nuclear conflict with each other. Those days are gone. Today's nuclear proliferators—India, Pakistan, China, North Korea, Japan's neighbors, in other words—do not share a common world vision; they are on collision courses with each other. Although the risks of a cataclysmic war between the major powers have receded, an Asian regional war is an ever-increasing possibility. Such a war could begin in Kashmir, in the Persian Gulf, on the Korean Peninsula or on Asia's busy sea-lanes. No matter what part of Asia it begins in, Japan would have to be involved.

Sunshine policies notwithstanding, arms control experts increasingly believe China, Pakistan, North Korea, Iran, and Syria have a clandestine network helping each other develop missiles in the face of international efforts to stop them. There is certainly remarkable similarities between the latest medium-range ballistic missiles tested by North Korea, Pakistan, and Iran. In geo-political terms, these covert alliances make the entire Asian region extremely volatile. In this connection, President Clinton's contentious statement that South Asia is currently the world's most dangerous place is still correct. Two historic enemies, India and Pakistan, after generations of mutual distrust, have now developed both nuclear weapons as well as the means to deliver them.

There are, of course, many other places in the world which are highly dangerous for the people who live there; the recent chaos in Chechnya, Afghanistan, and Syria are just some of the most recent such bloody events that speckle the pages of history. But those conflicts have either been contained or have only limited regional significance. That is not the situation in South Asia.

India and Pakistan must rank as the most likely candidates for a conflict that risks ultimately a nuclear confrontation. And in the background there is Pakistan's ally—China—which, with North Korea and its other vassal countries, has almost certainly helped Pakistan develop both its nuclear bomb and its rocket forces. India warily watches China; both countries have ambitions of playing a significant regional security role, and it is ultimately China's arsenal that is the reference point for Indian military planners as they modernize their own forces. The stakes are now that much higher in the entire region.

India and Pakistan have for their own security reasons broken with the widely supported nuclear non-proliferation regime, norms which they never entirely accepted. In going nuclear, they have provided a dangerous precedent for North Korea, Iran and other unstable countries to follow. North Korea and maybe even Iran could pose a ballistic missile threat to the continental United States within the near future. The most dangerous threat to the world is still the proliferation of weapons of mass destruction. And as a fully-fledged example of proliferation, South Asia has set a very worrying precedent. More to our point, Japan, the deployment of a token number of anti missile batteries in Tokyo notwithstanding, has not the means to defend itself against the threats nuclear and missile proliferation beget.

Japan, as the Aum and North Korean cases clearly show, is

singularly unprepared for whatever disasters China might bring her way. She can no longer depend on America. Nor can she depend on the Pax Americana. There is no tried and trusted way to avoid these conflicts. Iran cannot be bullied into acquiescence and China will not allow North Korea to be bribed into playing by the international rules. On current projects, India and Pakistan must eventually go to war again. The international chessboard is trickier than it has ever been and Japan is uniquely unsuited to play the game. Japanese foreign policy traditionally favored bilateral relations over complex multilateral interrelationships. Japan traditionally allied itself to a great power and alienated others in the process. Japan, for example, misunderstood the impact its alliance with Nazi Germany would have on its relationships with the United States. It failed to see that the Soviet Union was the wrong mediator to end the Pacific War and it lost the Northern Territories and 500,000 soldiers into Siberian slavery as a result.

Japan's current relationship with the United States is equally simplistic. It ignores the dynamics China in particular has brought into the Asian arena. Asia's dynamic forces will eventually impose onto Japan's vital interests unless Japan, in combination with the United States, begins to effect countermeasures now. Because it is one of the world's largest economies, Japan must play a fitting and constructive regional role.

Japan, in consort with the United States, must effect a Russian entente that incorporates China's interests as well. If it will not develop a nuclear arsenal, it must, at least, play a preeminent role in TMD. It must reinvigorate its arms industry and show China, India, and North Korea that it has the military teeth needed to veto any major Chinese-induced changes in the South China Sea, on the Korean peninsula, in Vietnam or anywhere else incompatible with its interests. If Japan is to be at the Asian negotiating table, it needs guns that speak louder than empty rhetoric. It needs to rearm.

America, as the world's preeminent power, will be faced with increasing challenges in the years ahead. India, Pakistan, and the Korean peninsula will keep the international order tense. If Russia relapses into anarchy, China and Iran could well follow. All of these countries see themselves as victims of the international order. All of them are prepared to push back—and cause another major world war in the process. Whether we are speaking of mainland Asia, Indonesia, India, or China itself, Japan will have to play a leading supportive role in ensuring the bush fires these countries fight along their borders do not turn into major hot wars. This will involve Japan having a formidable army, ready, willing and able to conduct a high tech war. Japan will have to play a role similar to that of Britain, Germany, and France play in the European arena. She must awake from her slumber.

Japan must be ready to put its soldiers into the frontline. Japan's occasional motions in the UN or its checkbook response to Iraq, East Timor and other emergencies are not enough. America's armed forces are not Japan's mercenaries. Japan has her vital interests to protect and, if all she can do is write a check, she cannot expect her hired guns to put their lives at risk for her. Unless Japan is prepared to see Japanese blood being spilled, unless Japan is prepared to see Japanese soldiers return to Japan in body bags, she cannot expect others to die for her interests. No appeals to her outmoded constitution can change that. Japan must rearm and take her rightful place in the world.

Although the prospect of a remilitarized Japan causes justified unease in Korea and China, this nervousness is unwarranted. Although Japan's days of empire are long since over, the political, military and economic challenges earlier chapters have outlined remain. Japan's days of isolation are likewise long since over and Japan will increasingly have to carry its load of the international community's global and regional problems. Japan's challenge is to be able to play such a leading political and military role without unduly antagonizing other countries, the PRC in particular. A proper defense strategy, coupled with a commitment to TMD, is the beginning of such a role.

This is, of course, assuming that Japan's neighbors do not uni-laterally disarm themselves and that Japan is not allowed to keep her head enmeshed in the sand for the next fifty years. It assumes, in other words, that Japan wants to mature and play its proper role in international affairs. It assumes that Japan must adopt a more assertive international role. If all of these assumptions are true, then Tokyo must continue its armed build-up within the param-eters of the American alliance and, at the same time, it must deepen its military contacts with South Korea and America's other regional allies. Although Japan will have to pay its fair share of the TMD program, these costs could be, in part at least, offset by Japan exporting her expertise in defensive weapons. It must carry its due share of the world's burdens and let the world know that it is carrying its fair share. Indeed, if Japan has been singularly weak in any one area, it has been in its inability to explain itself to the outside world. Japan not only carries a little stick but it never says anything. The world needs a Japan that can forcibly argue its cor-ner in the world's diplomatic corridors.

Japan must address this shortcoming as a matter of some urgency. The world thinks that Japan piggybacks on the American defense alliance and yet, in many ways, America piggybacks on Japan. North Korea, the PRC and Japan's other neighbors con-stantly harangue Japan about its past perfidies and Japan must hang its head in shame and under no circumstances point out their own considerable human rights shortcomings. Japan must export its produce to the world and obey the rules other nations have set. Japan must gear itself to be an export machine and suf-fer the propaganda flak such an over-exposure to the vagaries of international trade entails. Japan must not even pay due homage to its emasculated flag, lest foreign political opportunists object. Most of all, Japan must not build up its military capabilities. It must, therefore, emasculate large portions of its own industry, pay the United States to protect it and hope against hope that China allows her sea-lanes to forever remain open and unthreatened.

No other major nation has to do that. Japan is a large and populous nation with its own inalienable rights. Those rights—the right to life, liberty and the pursuit of happiness—have to be defended if they are attacked. Japan has an inalienable right to defend her people, her territorial integrity, and her rights of sea and air access. The fact that she is ill equipped to defend herself does not negate that right. It merely poses the question as to how Japan can develop that capability, given the array of constraints she must work under.

Because Japan today faces a more uncertain world, she must build her strategy around those factors she thinks are most beneficial and most stable to her own interests. The American link has been the most stable and beneficial factor behind the success Japan has enjoyed since 1945. Although America's regional power will continue to decline, it will be some years yet until China replaces America as East Asia's dominant power. This gives Japan the necessary time window to ensure that East Asia will evolve in a manner conducive to her own core needs. This will entail Japan fostering the links between herself, America and America's other regional allies. Japan has an inalienable right to deepen such alliances. It is up to Japan's diplomats to explain these needs both to the PRC and the world at large.

Japan must deepen those links and neutralize whatever spin the foreign mass media put on them. This will, in the first instance, entail Japan finally cleaning up the mess its imperial era bequeathed it. Japan must make amends once and for all for its past human rights transgressions. Japan already is the world's largest international aid donor. Some of those funds can be diverted to ease the old age of those who suffered the most from Japan's past aggressions. Such a fund catering to those needs could be expanded to incorporate all East Asians who have suffered aggression, from whatever source. These sources would include not only Japan and the United States, but Vietnam, North Korea, the PRC, Indonesia and other prominent Asian nations, too. The propaganda utility of such an exercise would be gained by getting the United States, South Korea, Taiwan and other countries to join in as minor contributors and by putting the fund under international supervision. Because such a program would go a long way to silencing Japan's critics, it would be worth it.

Japan's NGOs could also play a substantial role in administering such a fund in Cambodia, Vietnam, Laos, India, the Philippines and similar countries. So too, in fact, could many of Japan's major companies. The key to all of this would be to atone for Japan's past wrongs and to let the world—and Japan's Asian neighbors in particular—know that atonement was being made.

The PRC, Vietnam, Indonesia, and North Korea have considerable crimes to atone for themselves and the sad reality is that they have proved to be as slow to repent as have the more reactionary elements of Japanese society. This being so, any such move by Japan must also be accompanied by a visit to the dentist. Japan's foreign policy must have teeth and, if Japan does not have the fangs, she must acquire them. If the only language that tomorrow's Asia will understand comes from the barrel of a gun, Japan must relearn that language and be prepared to make her weapons bark.

Because the days of unilateral military action by Japan are over, she must rearm in consort with her allies, the United States in particular. This entails the development of the TMD program and a retention of most dual use technologies in Japan. The United States knows that she has carved modern Japan largely to suit her own needs. Japan has certain economic needs that must remain autonomous. These center on Japan's need to earn sufficient export revenue to maintain her economic independence. And that does not entail her going to war again.

Japan's economy is geared to paying any price, not carrying any burden, for the vital necessities the Japanese economy needs. Whereas the United States has demonstrated that the free flow of oil from the Persian Gulf is of such vital interest that she is prepared to go to war over it, Japan has been forced to sing a different tune. Japan's export-oriented economy is geared to earn the foreign currency Japan needs to buy oil, food, and the other staples she depends on. If America allows an expanding China, an imploding Indonesia or any other country to cut off those oil supplies, they must be prepared for whatever reaction Japan chooses to give.

Japan's checkbook can go a long way to neutralize these contingencies. It can help to pacify the northern border with Russia. It can help to make Russia a buffer against China. But in the end, the checkbook is not enough. Japan must rearm. She must develop a sword as well as the shield of TMD.

Given the challenges Japan will increasingly face, TMD without the prospects of abandonment or entrapment must be Japan's most favored choice. The United States has it within her power to deliver that choice to Japan. Allowing Japan to develop autonomously within the TMD umbrella would be merely a continuation of the status quo. This status quo has served both countries well. Its continuation would build on that happy history and would eventually bring the PRC and North Korea into the fold as well.

The alternative scenario suits nobody, Pyongyang's unstable leaders excepted. Japan has it within her power to create an alternative future more beneficial to everybody. Once her checkbook allows her to clear the residue of her imperialist past, she can then begin to play the more forthright role in international affairs her economic prowess demands. This will entail Japan taking up her full role in the United Nations and similar bodies. It will mean an increasingly internationalist focus for Japan's major companies and influential bodies. It will, ultimately, mean a more secure and successful future for Japan and her allies. Japan, today's toothless tiger, will, for the first time in its history, be able to play a role as an engine of economic growth in the world. And that will benefit everybody.

Land of the Risen Sun

Both China and Japan were dragged unwillingly into the Western socio-economic orbit. In the case of Japan, this occurred through a number of traumatic events, the most notable of which are the Meiji Restoration and the Second World War, which, at the time of writing, makes Japan unique in that it is the only country that was devastated by atomic weapons. Japan has paid her dues to the world in rivers of blood and atomized bodies. She is a fully paid up member of the international community with which she is in good standing and she is morally indebted to no one, least of all the People's Republic of China. She is a modern nation state with a variety of domestic and foreign challenges to meet on the economic, social, cultural, military, and diplomatic fronts and she would prefer to get on with those tasks than compete with China in an arms race.

Japan's star has therefore risen and has yet to wane—and Japan has no intention of letting it wane. Though she has shown her claws in the distant past, she would prefer to get on with the difficult job of building for the future than to trade blows with her giant neighbor. China, too, should look to the future and not keep peering through the biased lenses she uses to cherry pick the past. China, in making her own future, should realize she can pick her friends, her favorites and her pantomime villains but, like the rest of us, she cannot pick her neighbors. She can be a good neighbor or she can find out that troublesome, noisy and self-respecting neighbors such as Japan, India, Vietnam, Russia, and Korea can deal with neighbors from hell if they have to; and the bigger they are, the harder they fall. China has a condescending attitude to her neighbors, whom she has historically regarded as children beholden to her. She now thinks she is the new military kid on the block, the big bully everyone has to kowtow to. The Vietnamese disagree; they have disagreed for over a thousand years and they will disagree for another 10,000 years. So too will Japan, which has had to pussyfoot around on the international stage for the last seventy years.

The Japanese and Vietnamese understand China's twin problems of multiplication and division: though China has a big national income cake to share, once all 1.3 billion citizens get a piece, they can only each presently get little more than a crumb when the cake is divided; when a small, localized problem is magnified by 1.3 billion, it becomes a very big national problem. China's neighbors therefore understand that China's leaders face huge problems keeping the Middle Kingdom politically, socially, and economically stable and that ongoing economic growth either through cooperation or conflict is essential to achieve those aims.

But the Chinese should understand their neighbors as well. The world and, in particular, countries like Vietnam and Japan, are not theirs and they should stop encroaching on them. Although they say that good fences make good neighbors, aggressive navies make very bad ones. History shows that Vietnam, Korea, and Japan will never kowtow to China; given that China does not expect to lie prostrate again before other powers, why should she expect her neighbors to subjugate themselves to her?

China imperiously regards Vietnam and Korea as troublesome children because they do not march in step behind China. But the Vietnamese and Koreans behave as adults; it is the Chinese who need to grow up and they can do that either the hard and bloody way or the easy and bloodless way. Let's hope, even if it is against hope, for all our sakes, that China can eventually learn to be a good and responsible neighbor so that all of Asia's economic tigers can remain toothless.